DESIGNING

The School Leader's

PORTFOLIO

SECOND EDITION

DESIGNING

The School Leader's

PORTFOLIO

SECOND EDITION

Mary E. Dietz

FOREWORD BY LINDA LAMBERT

CORWIN PRESS
A SAGE Company
Thousand Oaks, CA 91320

For information:
Corwin Press

A SAGE Company
2455 Teller Road
Thousand Oaks, California 91320
www.corwinpress.com

SAGE Ltd.
1 Oliver's Yard
55 City Road
London, EC1Y 1SP
United Kingdom

SAGE India Pvt. Ltd.
B 1/I 1 Mohan Cooperative
Industrial Area
Mathura Road, New Delhi 110 044
India

SAGE Asia-Pacific Pte. Ltd.
33 Pekin Street #02-01
Far East Square
Singapore 048763

Printed in the United States of America

Library of Congress Cataloging-in-Publication Data
Dietz, Mary E.
  Designing the school leader's portfolio / Mary E. Dietz ; foreword by Linda Lambert. — 2nd ed.
    p. cm.
  Includes bibliographical references and index.
  ISBN 978-1-4129-4895-1 (cloth) — ISBN 978-1-4129-4896-8 (pbk.)
  1. School administrators—In-service training. 2. Portfolios in education. I. Title.
  LB1738.5.D54 2008
  371.2'011—dc22
                                            2007040313
This book is printed on acid-free paper.

07 08 09 10 11 10 9 8 7 6 5 4 3 2 1

Acquisitions Editor: Hudson Perigo
Editorial Assistants: Jodan Barbakow, Lesley Blake
Production Editor: Appingo Publishing Services
Cover Designer: Scott Van Atta

Contents

Foreword

How do leaders learn? Our profession has thought deeply about teacher learning. Beyond preparation, we support new teachers, pursue reflective practice, engage in instructional supervision and coaching, and design professional development. Indeed, thinking about teacher learning is one of our major preoccupations. This is as it should be.

However, we have not given the same attention to a formal leader's learning. Beyond preparation, the professional development of administrators is haphazard, scant, random, and dependent on the flourishing of such endeavors as leadership academies or institutes. Learning that is systematically embedded in practice is elusive for most formal leaders. Those who are naturally thoughtful carve out their own learning plans and strategies; those who are less thoughtful or view leadership as reactionary rarely engage in systematic learning.

Is there something about the nature of leadership or of the job itself that warrants such neglect? Have leaders already learned what there is to learn? Hardly. In this book, Mary E. Dietz offers us a synthesis of current notions of leadership that helps us to understand that this work requires wisdom, compelling ideas, explicit values and vision, and the shared construction of meaning. Leading is moral work involving "the willingness to be accountable for the well-being of the larger organization by operating in service of those around us" (Block, 1993). Intriguingly, Dietz translates this transformative work into standards that draw out the skills and understandings of leadership. This discussion sets the stage for the real work to come.

In *Designing the School Leader's Portfolio,* Dietz has created a process and a framework that significantly improve the chances that administrators will learn within the context of leading. Such learning requires that district, school, and personal/professional goals and aims converge. Further, alignment among processes for assessing children, teachers, and administrators comes together for the first time. This convergence, or intersection, enables leaders to make sense of their work and find authenticity in shared purpose. This participatory process is a vehicle for the systemic design of an engaging, portfolio development journey—for portfolio is a verb more than it is a noun.

Four phases of the portfolio design frame, a comprehensive learning process, are

- purpose, creating clarity about philosophy and leadership;
- focus, zeroing in on goals and a banner question;
- process, creating plans, gathering artifacts and evidence, participating in professional development activities and roundtable discussions;
- outcomes, assessing and articulating what is learned.

The banner question is a particularly noteworthy concept. This essential or focusing question frames the context for learning. Such a question provides an entry point into the inquiry process, often bubbling into other questions that lead to surprises and new understandings. Collaboration is thoughtful work with portfolio partners (peer coaches) and teams in a roundtable format.

If the portfolio process were presented as a singular journey, it would not be in step with current and persistent thinking that leadership is a shared endeavor. Because of the highly participatory nature of this process, it tends to build learning communities of educational leaders. Leaders experience themselves as learners, collaborators, and facilitators of community learning. This learning container ensures that the best that we know about professional learning takes place: reflection, inquiry, dialogue, and action.

This book is replete with examples, graphics, tools, logs, registries, and questions that bring the text to life. It is highly useable. This book can guide those who have responsibility for the preparation and professional development of school leaders. It can stand on its own.

Dietz has created

- a pioneering effort in the field of leading and learning,
- a comprehensive system that incorporates state of the art assessment endeavors, and
- a learning process.

Congratulations are in order for work well done and skillfully applied in the field through her experiences in districts large and small, urban and suburban.

All leaders learn (just like children). As Dietz points out, "The portfolio provides an envelope for the mind that gives both framework and process to the learner." This work builds a rapprochement between leader and learner that takes us beyond our current experience.

Linda Lambert
Professor Emeritus
Department of Educational Leadership
California State University, Hayward

How to Use
This Book

Designing the School Leader's Portfolio is a practical guide and resource for establishing a clear purpose and process to inform and facilitate leadership development. The leadership performance system (LPS) has a structure and process that is easily adapted to accommodate individual and organizational needs such as leadership, evaluation, credentialing, professional learning communities, targeted professional development, and supporting lateral leadership in the school system.

The LPS is organized around four phases—purpose, focus, process, and outcomes. Chapters 2 through 5 include the steps for designing and participating in the LPS process as you move through the four phases. Specific activities and protocols for the four phases are included in these chapters.

The book includes the LPS Resource Matrix, page xi, aligning the collection of tools and other resources that inform and facilitate the portfolio design and implementation. These resources are organized around the four LPS phases—purpose, focus, process and outcomes. In keeping with the digital era a CD is also provided to support the customized construction of your "desktop" digital portfolio. Details of how to optimize technology throughout the portfolio process are addressed in Chapter 6.

CHAPTER BY CHAPTER ■

Chapter 1 "The Role of the Leadership Performance System in Accelerating Student Achievement" describes the LPS and how it works as a system with interdependent elements, all contributing to the professional development and capacity building of leadership in your school district.

Examples of key activities that align with student achievement include

- Set goals and build action plans with check points to monitor progress,
- assess current state and student data to determine instructional goals, and
- participate in leadership professional learning community activities.

These critical activities are organized, focused, and examined through the reflective, collaborative process of the LPS. Chapter 1 introduces the four phases of the portfolio process and stresses the need to define leadership and the key attributes of school leaders.

Chapter 2, "Establishing a Purpose for the LPS," introduces the first of the four phases, purpose. Leaders use this chapter as a starting point for reaching an agreement regarding the purpose and function of the LPS in their school community. After agreeing on the purpose, leaders set expectation for performance outcomes and consider the use of standards such as the ISLLC standards.

Chapter 3, "Focusing the LPS," addresses the second phase of the process, focus. In "Focusing the LPS," leaders find the tools to establish the goals and specific learning outcomes for the school, the students, and the leader. During the focus phase, leaders identify the set of performance standards for their LPS work and generate a banner question, an essential question that becomes their primary focus for learning and work for the year. This question provides the focus by guiding the selection of learning activities and collection of artifacts and evidence.

Once they have established a purpose and focus for the portfolio, leaders move to the collaboration phase. Chapters 4 and 5 address the structures and processes for establishing a leadership professional learning community and the action planning process.

Chapter 4, "The Process and Structures for Collaborations," addresses the professional structures that will support the LPS collaborations. Structures such as leadership roundtables, leadership professional learning communities and identifying an LPS "partner" all contribute to establishing leaders collaboration network to support the professional development process.

Chapter 5, "Outcomes for Action Planning and Reporting Results," describes action-planning component of the process phase, in which leaders plan their learning activities, actions, and partnerships for reflection and professional collaboration. The chapter offers tools to assist in scheduling and facilitating roundtable discussions to share progress and learning within the LPS process.

All of the activities in the first three phases prepare school administrators for the final reflection and sharing of artifacts, evidence, and learning in the fourth phase of the LPS, outcomes.

The fourth and final phase of the LPS process is the outcome phase. This phase explains when leaders summarize their learning and plan their next steps.

Chapter 6, "Technology and the LPS Process," contains a technology resource guide with suggestions for using technology to enhance and streamline the portfolio process.

It includes the LPS Resource Matrix that align with the four phases of the LPS process. The LPS CD contains links to resources and a digital copy of the LPS Journal. This document can be used to customize your LPS and to record planning steps, share progress with colleagues, and archive short- and long-term results.

LPS Resource Matrix

A Guide to Resources and Templates

RESOURCES	PURPOSE	FOCUS	PROCESS	OUTCOMES
LPS Portfolio Journal (See CD)	√	√	√	√
Leadership Performance System Model pp. xxiv, 70	√	√	√	√
ISLLC Standards and LPS Alignment pp. 3, 19	√	√	√	√
Technology Resource Guide p. 65	√	√	√	√
LPS Phases Process p. 69	√	√	√	√
Steps in the LPS Process p. 71	√	√	√	√
ISLLC Standards Resources p. 93	√	√	√	
TEMPLATES				
Steps in the LPS Process p. 71	√	√	√	√
Agreement on Purpose p. 74	√	√		
Defining Your Theory of Action p. 75	√	√		
Focused Leadership p. 76	√			
Establishing Targeted Priority Goals p. 77	√	√		
Banner Question Template p. 78		√		
Professional Structures for Collaboration Survey p. 79	√	√	√	
Professional Development Activities Log p. 80			√	
Evidence Registry p. 81			√	√
Outcomes of the LPS Process p. 82				√

√ Indicates alignment with portfolio phases; a valuable tool for users

Acknowledgments

I would like to take this opportunity to recognize the school communities that have contributed learnings that are reflected in the leadership portfolio design and process: the New York City Teacher Centers Consortium; the Acalanes High School District, Pleasant Hill, California; and the Saratoga Union School District, Saratoga, California. Through our shared experiences, we defined and refined the role of the portfolio in assessing and building capacity for school leaders to facilitate an environment that has an impact on student learning.

My early work in the Shoreham-Wading River (New York) school district served to build a foundation for my professional learning community that is still vital today.

I would also like to acknowledge Linda Lambert for writing the foreword and Bonnie Keast for assisting with the manuscript refining process.

Among the most influential mentors in my life has been my husband, Tom, who offers guidance, feedback, suggestions, and encouragement. His constant encouragement and cheerleading have been an inspiration.

—*Mary E. Dietz*

About the Author

Mary E. Dietz is an international consultant and former president and cofounder of LearnCity, a company dedicated to serving educators with a systemswide solution for designing, delivering, and assessing standards-based instruction using the power of technology.

 Ms. Dietz's career as a consultant began in 1989 when she established Frameworks for Learning Organizations. Prior to that she taught special education and served as a reading specialist for Grades K–8. Her consulting practice is focused on assisting educational leaders in building their internal capacity for organizing and facilitating learning communities in school systems.

She has coached teachers, administrators, school boards, district and site leadership teams, and communities in establishing the collaborations and relationships necessary for systemic change. Much of her work with educators has been in the areas of systems design, strategic planning, professional development, coaching, and alternative assessments for educators.

Ms. Dietz is the founder of the National Staff Development Council's *Network for Portfolio Users* and is a member of the design team for establishing a Network for Educational Coaching in California. Most recently she served as the lead designer and facilitator in establishing an online knowledge management system for implementing standards-based instruction in California.

Introduction

WHAT IS THE LEADERSHIP PERFORMANCE SYSTEM? ■

The leadership performance system (LPS) provides a framework for initiating, planning, and facilitating ongoing professional growth while connecting the purpose and focus of the leader, the district/school, and the school community. It is an organizer for reflection and learning. The LPS provides a structure and process to assist school leaders in their efforts to be high performing leaders, building, and sustaining a culture of collaboration and continuous improvement. The LPS focuses goal setting, action plans, and professional learning for the educational leader. In addition, the LPS contributes to building a professional learning community that encourages peer collaborations in school systems, where the standards and evaluation system function as a tool for professional development. The LPS coaches, or facilitates, the process to optimize learning and collaboration on the part of the school leader.

WHO NEEDS LPS? ■

The LPS process is designed for any person with a leadership role in a school system including principals and school and district administrators. Some school systems use the LPS as part of the administrator evaluation and credentialing process; others invite school leaders to use the LPS for individual and group planning and learning; and some school leaders use the process to plan, collaborate, and self-assess. Any combination of these purposes fits with the LPS design, but it is important for school leaders to clarify the purpose and function of their engagement at the beginning of the process.

The first reaction of most school leaders to the suggestion that they engage in this process is "I don't have time to fit one more task into my schedule." But participating in the LPS process that this book describes is not an additional task—it is an activity that informs and focuses all of the school leader's tasks, making the school leader more efficient in all that he or she does.

The time commitment is minimal—frequent informal meetings with an LPS partner over coffee, breakfast, or lunch, and a monthly roundtable session of one to two hours. In between, the process demands only reflection, focused thinking, and data collection. The LPS process actually reduces the time school leaders spend making decisions or carrying out school plans.

The LPS provides tools and resources to assist leaders in using the process for their performance review and professional learning. The tools guide their reflection and group discussion. LPS participants do not work alone. They share the process with a partner and a roundtable group—peer coaches who aid in every step of the process by offering feedback, ideas, and their own experience.

Educators around the globe have used this process to organize, focus, and facilitate their professional work and learning. To date, the process has been studied and documented in at least eleven doctoral dissertations. The process continues to evolve as educators contribute their ideas and successes and modify and enhance each phase.

■ BENEFITS OF LPS

The LPS can have the traditional focus of standards-based self-assessment and/or administrator evaluation, a record of meeting credentialing requirements and ongoing professional development, or a record of accomplishments for future employment. Throughout the process, the leader can combine aspects of the professional performance plan and self-assessment, and, as such, it builds one's capacity for leadership.

As a means of organizing the information, goals, and evidence toward meeting goals, the leader can develop a portfolio—a "container" of sorts to organize materials related to formal district evaluation as self-assessment. The very process of assembling a portfolio focuses the school leader's goals and objectives. In addition, the portfolio tracks improvement of leadership qualities and encourages peer discussion and evaluation as well as collaborative learning.

■ THE STEPS OF THE LPS PROCESS

The LPS participants move through the five interdependent phases of the LPS process:

- Purpose and function for leadership work—establish purpose for the LPS
- Focus for learning—focus the LPS and connect schoolwide, and districtwide goals
- Structures for collaboration—identify groups (or structures) that provide the context for the process (i.e., boards, leadership groups, administrators' groups, district roundtables)
- Action planning—engage in learning activities and collaborate with peers, collect data and evidence
- Outcomes for improvement—assess and exhibit outcomes

This book supports recommendations with examples and real-life situations of how the LPS can make the school leader more effective and a colearner with colleagues. It offers a step-by-step process for facilitating and focusing learning.

DEFINING AN EFFECTIVE SCHOOL LEADER ■

The LPS can help clarify the school leader's goals, strengths, and weaknesses and contribute to his or her effective leadership. But what qualities make an effective leader?

Leaders in an educational system must have the ability to zoom in and zoom out; that is, leaders must be able to step back and look at the big picture to determine the impact of decisions, mandates, or innovations. Then they must have the ability to shift their focus to the details and again step back to view the big picture. For example, deciding whether to move to a block schedule requires consideration of the following: How do block schedules impact instructional time? Are transportation and other services flexible enough to accommodate the change? Does the change have the support of teachers, parents, community members, and curriculum designers? Most important, what are the benefits of this effort?

It is up to the administrator to coordinate and prioritize all activities and allocate resources in response to student needs, mandates, and community priorities. Administrators must build capacity and commitment among staff members to increase student success. According to Linda Lambert (1998), conditions for building that capacity are as follows:

1. Hire personnel with the proved capacity to do leadership work, and develop veteran staff to become skillful leaders.

2. Get to know one another to build trusting relationships.

3. Assess staff and school capacity for leadership. Do staff members have a shared purpose? Do they work collaboratively? Is there a schoolwide focus on student achievement?

4. Develop a culture of inquiry that includes a continuous cycle of reflecting, questioning, gathering evidence, and planning for improvements.

5. Organize for leadership work by establishing inclusive governance structures and collaborative inquiry processes.

6. Implement plans for building leadership capacity, and anticipate role changes and professional development needs.

7. Develop district policies and practices that support leadership capacity building. The district should model the processes of a learning organization.

DEFINING LEADERSHIP: VOICES OF WISDOM ■

Before beginning their process of defining standards for and attributes and expectations of educational leaders, members of one group of educational leaders explored leadership definitions. They looked to the following voices of wisdom that describe their values and purpose as leaders and discuss constructing a learning organization (an environment where one learns and improves continually through experiences and new information), building a sense of community, and recognizing the school as an evolving system.

Cile Chavez (1992), a past superintendent, stated, "My role isn't so much to make things happen but to make sense of things, to show how things fit together." To her, a leader is less about doing than being. Her messages of meaning encourage others to seek focus and mission in their work. Sharing this search gives purpose and direction to the school as a system with its members all working together toward common, shared goals.

Thomas Sergiovanni (1993) spoke of redefining leadership. The essence of the revised definition is the importance of the concepts, values, and ideals one brings to the practice of leadership. While management skills and competence remain important and help smooth the way, leaders must rely less on their people-handling skills and more on offering compelling ideas in the form of a mission and purpose others can share. The two banners of mission and purpose leading the way position the school to be more agile in responding to continual change in student needs and the effects the changing needs have on the school as a system.

Chavez (1992) and Sergiovanni (1993) highlighted the necessity of leaders to align who they are with what they do. Their words invite leaders to focus on their higher purpose of leader as observer, engineer, composer, and facilitator rather than merely manager. Leaders set purpose, focus goals and outcomes, and establish feedback loops to monitor progress and continual learning for improvements. Chavez and Sergiovanni stressed the need to build commitment in the school community rather than monitor compliance. In today's work environment, compliance will not help educators meet the demands of the Information Age and lifelong learning. The revised model of leadership emphasizes the leader's role of facilitating and organizing the work of the system with all participants contributing to the shared purpose, mission, and vision rather than merely complying with a manager's ideas. Leadership is more than managing the tasks at hand; it is focusing participants and building their capacity to improve continually. A leader's philosophy, purpose, values, and beliefs are at the forefront of his or her work. The LPS process gives leaders the opportunity to construct their philosophy and purpose.

As another voice of wisdom, Arnold Packer (1992) saw the school as a system serving the community as well as serving the future employment needs of the community. He stressed the importance of shared purpose and agreement of focus as an essential element to enable a school system to move forward. Because it helps school leaders align their goals with schoolwide and districtwide plans, the LPS process integrates and focuses the goals and shared purpose of educational leaders with that of their system.

The essential element of shared purpose is a foundation for community, with all members sharing in the responsibility to achieve results. The reciprocal processes of constructivist leadership enable participants in an educational community to construct meanings that lead toward a common purpose about schooling (Lambert, Collay, & Dietz, 1995).

Packer (1992) also highlighted the necessity of shared purpose. The LPS process begins with school leaders defining their purpose and philosophy in an effort to build a foundation for the goal setting and learning that will follow. In addition, the LPS is structured around goals, outcomes, and a process for interpreting data related to student learning, connecting the leaders' school plan with district goals and their own professional development.

Peter Senge (1990) identified a critical element of a learning organization: "The development of collective meaning is an essential characteristic of a learning organization" (p. 241). He stated further,

> The leader's new work for the future is building learning organizations. This new view of leadership in learning organizations centers on subtler and more important tasks. In a learning organization, leaders are designers, stewards, and teachers. They are responsible for building organizations where people continually expand their capabilities to understand complexity, clarify vision, and improve shared mental models—that is, they are responsible for learning. (p. 340)

According to Senge (1990), many of the best intentioned efforts to foster new learning disciplines flounder because those leading the charge forget the first rule of learning: people learn when they need to learn, not when someone else thinks they need to learn.

In *Renewing America's Schools,* Carl Glickman (1993) discussed the need for disequilibrium in a school system. When learners experience disequilibrium, the unrest that occurs when they face a situation or information that does not make sense to them, they attempt to accommodate the new ideas or situation by calling on past experiences and interactions with people, objects, and ideas to build new understandings. The unrest in a school system that occurs on examination of student learning data leads educational leaders to ask questions such as "why are we getting these results?" and "what should our focus and goals be to impact a change in outcomes?" Without disequilibrium, learning and improvement do not occur. One would never ask questions such as "why is this happening?" and "how can I influence change?" Glickman offered the following example of how wisdom and the notion of a learning organization serve educational leaders in moving forward and seeking new results:

> Success is the intelligent use of mistakes in self-renewing schools. The moral imperative of the school is for its members to move into their areas of incompetence: if we already know exactly how to do this work, we should not have the purposeless cycles of educational reform that schools are endlessly caught in. We all need to learn new roles and relationships. (p. 91)

The LPS process encourages reflection on and examination of data as evidence of what works and what does not work to improve student learning.

Michael Fullan (1991) stressed the challenge of decision making in regard to school change initiatives:

> The greatest problem faced by school districts and schools is not resistance to innovation, but the fragmentation, overload, and incoherence resulting from the uncritical and uncoordinated acceptance

of too many different innovations. Changes abound in the schools of today. The role of the district is to help schools sort out and implement the right choices. (p. 197)

Through the LPS process, educational leaders examine their process in new ways.

Peter Block (1993) stressed the need for letting go of the need to control through structures by challenging leaders to look at the key element for change. He stated, "If there is no transformation inside of us, all the structural change in the world will have no impact on our institution" (p. 44). Block promoted stewardship, which he defined as the willingness to be accountable for the well-being of the larger organization by operating in service of others rather than controlling them. Because stewardship requires leaders to choose service over self-interest, it requires a level of trust most leaders are not used to holding. Stewardship requires that leaders be accountable for the outcomes of the institution without acting to define purpose for others, control others, or take care of others. The LPS process is designed to support and facilitate collaboration and, thus, build a learning community among the school leadership and, in turn, throughout the school community. Having an LPS partner and participating in LPS roundtable discussions contribute to building and sustaining a learning community.

Margaret Wheatley (1992) challenged leaders to adapt and to be active learners facilitating a learning community:

> I believe that we have only just begun the process of discovering and inventing the new organizational formula that will inhabit the twenty-first century. To be responsible inventors and discoverers, though, we need the courage to let go of the old world, to relinquish most of what we cherished, to abandon our interpretations about what does and doesn't work. As Einstein is often quoted as saying: "No problem can be solved from the same consciousness that created it. We must learn to see the world anew." (p. 5)

The LPS process invites and encourages building learning communities by providing leaders collaborative structures and processes through which they support each other's efforts to become more adaptable. The section that follows provides a review of the background and theoretical underpinnings that drive current understanding of the school as a system and the leader's role and function in that system.

■ THE EVOLVING ROLE OF EDUCATIONAL LEADERSHIP

As we move through this new century and consider the challenges facing school systems, it is important to consider the role of leadership in guiding school communities in their mission of education. How will leaders grow professionally in their demanding and ever-changing role? Participation in the LPS process that aligns goals and enhances collaboration contributes strongly to preparing leaders for the challenges of the twenty-first century.

If learning communities are to be vehicles for processing and responding to the accelerated rate of change in the Information Age, how will leaders build the capacity and commitment for responding to change? The LPS offers both a structure and a process for building learning communities among educational leaders. Participation in the LPS process allows leaders to model and experience three of their critical roles: leader as learner, leader as collaborator, and leader as facilitator of learning communities.

The terms *learning organization* and *learning communities* are used with increasing frequency in educational systems. The emergence of learning in an organizational sense is the realization that change has become the norm. Educational systems no longer implement a program, evaluate it for three years, and then consider next steps. The pace has been accelerated to the point where constant change is the norm. Educational leaders seek models to assist them in finding and maintaining the balance between the chaos of rapid change and order.

KEY ELEMENTS OF ORGANIZING SCHOOL SYSTEMS ■

In *Leadership and the New Science,* Margaret Wheatley (1992) combined the concepts of learning communities and evolving systems. Her work with systems cites four key elements involved in organizing and focusing growing school systems: chaos, information, relationships, and vision/purpose. Wheatley compared mechanical systems such as a car with living systems such as an ocean or lake. In mechanical systems, outside forces both break down and repair the system. A mechanical system has limited potential; living systems, on the other hand, have the potential to revive, grow, and evolve. They are sensitive to environmental changes such as lack of nourishment and vulnerable to dysfunction such as the addition of toxic waste.

In school systems, many environmental changes impact the work; yet, they are outside the system's scope of control. For example, a change in funding, community priorities, or state or federal agency demands can affect the function of the system. These changes require adjustments within the system, but they are not under the immediate control of the system. Balance within the system is necessary to sustain efforts and commitments and respond effectively to the mandates, demands, and changes.

Chaos

Wheatley (1992) also offered guidelines for thriving in a world of change and chaos. Chaos is often caused by the rapid rate of change in a living system. Chaos is a process by which natural systems, including organizations, renew, and revitalize themselves. Accepting chaos is essential. Just as disequilibrium is essential to promote learning, chaos is an essential part of the learning organization. It is through the chaos of new mandates, competing needs, and constant changes that the organization continually seeks to clarify, focus, and understand as it attempts to respond appropriately.

As people move through the process of chaos, new levels of understanding emerge and the system finds a new equilibrium. Systems have the potential to self-organize and self-reorganize to adapt to environmental changes. Leaders need to embrace that tension between order and chaos in the evolving system and accept it as an essential part of the process of system growth.

Resistance is usually the initial response to change. First, there is doubt the change will really occur; then when it does occur, there is uncertainty about whether the new way can be a success. Self-esteem falters as staff members become concerned about potential changes in job titles and responsibilities. Individuals who can move out of this initial resistance are open to the flow of new information and can search for understanding and thus accommodate the chaos. This reaction actually causes more chaos, but it is through this continual process that the system reorganizes itself and moves to a new sense of order. In response to a need or mandate, the system is renewed as it incorporates new practices and programs.

Information

Successful living systems must have information (Wheatley, 1992). Sharing information is an essential organizing force in any organization because information guides and drives decisions. The more members of the system share the information, the better the chance of having new understandings systemwide. Test score data, new standards, research pertaining to learning, and strategies for meeting individual student needs are examples of shared information. This information informs the continually evolving system.

A major challenge is to refine and combine the new ideas without overburdening the system. In other words, letting go of old ways as new ideas and information are included refines the work rather than simply adding more pieces.

Information both forms and informs the system. For information to flow in the organization, trusting relationships, a shared purpose, and clear understanding of each person's intention must exist. The integration of old and new ways requires a willingness to let go of the attitude that states, "This is the way we always do things around here!" By establishing norms for the continuous flow of information within the organization, the leader ensures an environment that recognizes information as an essential element for vitality.

Relationships

The third essential attribute in a living system, according to Wheatley (1992), is relationships. A rich diversity of relationships is needed to energize teams. Relationships are the core of the system. If relationships work, the work goes well; if relationships do not work, the work does not go well. One of the most essential roles a leader plays is creating an environment where trusting professional relationships grow and are nurtured. Conversing about shared purposes, studying together, and learning and problem solving together form the glue that sustains a learning community. Professional relationships provide a bond that sustains focus in the system during times of chaos. The more supportive the relationships are, the greater the richness and diversity of ideas and understandings are and the greater the commitment to a shared purpose is.

Vision and Purpose

The last essential attribute of a healthy system is vision and shared purpose (Wheatley, 1992). Leaders must embrace vision as the invisible field that can enable the organization to recreate the workplace and the world. Although vision pulls the whole organization forward, it is not a final destination. The field of vision forms and reforms as the school moves toward a shared purpose and goal. A good starting point is defining the organization's shared purpose and building actions to move forward. Moving forward means understanding, checking in with members of the system, and assessing the success indicators, then continually refining the process. It is the leader's task to create a sense of stability in the unstable environment and to orient others in the system where knowledge is temporary and change is the norm.

Shared purpose and continual improvements are also reflected in Senge's (1990) definition of learning communities. He defined learning communities as

> [G]roups of individuals who have come together with a shared purpose and agree to construct new understandings…a place where people continually expand their capacity to create the results they truly desire, where new and expansive patterns of thinking are nurtured, where collective aspiration is set free, and where people are continually learning how to learn together. (p. 241)

An understanding of organizational learning communities and of how systems evolve helps leaders establish their own focus and role in the school system. Leaders are primarily responsible for

- managing the balance between order and chaos;
- establishing shared purpose, focus, and goals;
- building and sustaining learning communities with trusting professional relationships;
- sustaining a level of high standards and expectations for all members of the learning community;
- facilitating the process of information flow throughout the system.

The LPS process assists educational leaders in building professional learning communities. The process gives them an opportunity to practice "systems watching" as they seek to recognize and develop a capacity to include Wheatley's (1992) four essential attributes of an evolving system. Leaders model the process and establish a professional norm for the system. They set an expectation by example of ongoing professional learning, collaboration, and commitment to continual improvements. Thus leaders advance the purpose and mission for education in the community while they respond to individual student needs and incorporate standards for excellence.

Figure 0.1   Leadership Performance System

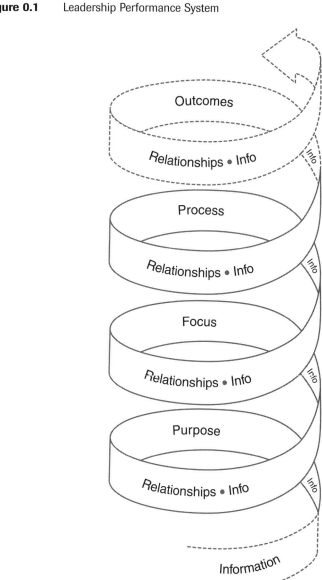

Figure 0.1 depicts the relationship between the systemwide change model and the LPS process. The flow of information that forms and informs the system requires trusting relationships, a shared purpose, and clear goals. Through its phases of purpose, focus, process, and outcomes, the LPS sets the stage for each of the elements essential for change.

In the purpose phase, school leaders define the LPS purpose in relation to their personal goals as well as district expectations; in other words, they determine a shared purpose. In the focus phase, leaders establish goals for the school, the students, and their own professional growth. In the process phase, leaders build the relationships so necessary to change as they establish a collaborative process and work with their peers to achieve the goals they have established. Finally, leaders use information they have accumulated to determine the outcomes of their efforts and set new goals for continuous improvement.

The Role of the Leadership Performance System in Accelerating Student Achievement

THE ROLE OF THE LEADERSHIP ■
PERFORMANCE SYSTEM

The leadership performance system (LPS) helps sustain personal and professional improvement by offering a system that aligns leadership performance and learning in the context of their school system. It provides school leaders with a contextual leadership assessment process (Figure 1.1). In a coherent and systematic way, it helps to compile and record goals, action plans, and data with deliberate attention to professional performance and evidence of effectiveness. As the means of organizing and streamlining evaluation, the LPS helps school leaders focus their goals for student learning, determine tools for evaluating student data, and establish professional priorities. Most important of all the LPS provides a structure and process to build capacity to support and sustain a leadership professional learning community.

Over the years I have depended on my own professional learning communities for reflection, collaboration, and filling in the blind spot in my thinking. Learning communities give me perspectives I have not yet accessed and pose challenging questions as to why, what, and how I am growing with my work. Most important, learning communities lead me to resources for expanding, deepening, and restructuring my understandings of the work of educators and the purpose of education in the Information Age. Without the combination of experiences from my various learning communities, I would never have matured in my understandings with the combination of conviction, confidence, and verve for my work. This combination of evolving knowledge, skills, values, and attitudes regarding work is developed and enhanced through the reflective collaborations with colleagues.

Creating the leadership portfolio is not just another activity; rather, it is an opportunity to advance goals, develop action plans, and provide evidence and outcomes in the context of a professional learning community.

Figure 1.1   The LPS

Leadership Performance System

Aligning Goals for Contextual Leadership

Outcomes/Results

School Plans/Goals

Leadership Assessment

Professional Collaborations
Capacity Building

Leadership Performance

For the past several years, national organizations, state departments of education, and local school leadership organizations have developed standards meant to align educational leaders with our changing and challenging times. Many states have adopted the Interstate School Leaders Licensure Consortium (ISLLC) standards to define the extensive scope of work and establish expectations for local administrators' practices. These standards provide a common language across state and regional differences, facilitating joint projects and sharing of effective strategies and resources.

The ISLLC standards place emphasis on leadership for student learning, which is central to school improvement and the current expectations of

No Child Left Behind (NCLB). Those standards articulate what administrators should know, believe, and be able to do to improve schools, increase student learning, and attend to the accountability requirements for student achievement. (See Appendix E for a complete list of the ISLLC standards.)

In 1994 and 1995, representatives from states and professional associations in partnership with the National Policy Board for Educational Administration wrote ISLLC's "Standards for School Leaders." The standards development was supported by grants from the Pew Charitable Trusts and the Danforth Foundation. They were published by the Council of Chief State School Officers (CCSSO) in 1996 and have been adopted or used by many states in the development of their own administrator standards and licensing policies (Figure 1.2).

Figure 1.2

ISLLC Standards and LPS in Alignment

ISLLC STANDARD	LEADERSHIP PERFORMANCE SYSTEM
Standard 1 A school administrator is an educational leader who promotes the success of all students by **facilitating the development, articulation, implementation, and stewardship of a vision** of learning that is shared and supported by the school community.	**PURPOSE** Leadership reflection of values, beliefs, and commitment–*Credo* **FOCUS** Priorities for action and for professional learning Employ systems planning model Use communication conventions
Standard 2 A school administrator is an educational leader who promotes the success of all students by **advocating, nurturing, and sustaining a school culture and instructional program** conducive to student learning and staff professional growth.	**PURPOSE** Alignment of vision, mission, and goals **PROCESS/STRUCTURES** Culture assessments, for reform readiness Review and establish professional learning community Relationships–roles and responsibilities Professional development for job-embedded learning Establish performance and professional learning goals
Standard 3 A school administrator is an educational leader who promotes the success of all students by ensuring management of the **organization, operations, and resources for a safe, efficient, an effective learning environment**.	**FOCUS/STRUCTURES** Alignment of goals and performance standards, identification of professional learning structure for completing work such as board, district leadership, leadership roundtable **PROCESS** Monitoring progress and making adaptations in planning as indicated **OUTCOMES** Determine action priorities Establish decision-making processes and communication conventions Practices to promote a theory of action

Figure 1.2 Continued

ISLLC STANDARD	LEADERSHIP PERFORMANCE SYSTEM
Standard 4 A school administrator is an educational leader who promotes the success for all students by **collaborating with families and community members, responding to diverse community interests, and needs, and mobilizing community resources**.	**PROCESS** Establish committees, focus groups, and parent advisories, identification of professional learning structure for completing the work such as school site council, parent groups, business/leadership roundtable Use meeting conventions and sustain active communications **OUTCOMES** Outreach to stakeholders, community, and board Engagement in action priorities
Standard 5 A school administrator is an educational leader who promotes the success of all students by **acting with integrity, fairness, an in an ethical manner.**	**PURPOSE** Clear purpose of the role of educational leadership in their community Commitment to honor shared and diverse values of the school community and the community at large **PROCESS** Employ professional efficacy and ethical frameworks to lead by example with exemplar ethical behaviors for the educational community
Standard 6 A school administrator is an educational leader who promotes the success for all students by **understanding, responding to, and influencing the larger political, social, economic, legal, and cultural context**.	**PURPOSE** Communicate vision and mission **PROCESS/STRUCTURES** Sustain outreach structures for convening the stakeholder group/identification of professional learning structure for completing the work—that is, board, district leadership, local government/leadership roundtable Establish a sustainable communication process with stakeholders **OUTCOMES** Professional network and learning community System planning procedures Report results and plan for continuous improvement Integrate new learning and feedback into practice

Most evaluations of school administrators are based on six primary performance areas, aligned with ISLLC's standards and tied to accelerating student learning:

- Articulate and facilitate a shared vision that represents community needs and aligns with goals for the school's student performance outcomes.
- Nurture a collaborative school culture and cohesive instructional program.
- Manage the organization and operations that sustain an efficient, safe, and effective environment.
- Mobilize collaborations among school, community, and business partners to optimize resources and expertise.
- Model professional ethics and highlight learning and commitment.
- Understand political, economic, and legal environments and respond in a professional manner that is in the interest of the local educational system.

(For background on the ISLLC standards, go to the CCSSO Web site: http://www.ccsso.org/content/pdfs/isllcstd.pdf.)

Of course, these six performance areas overlap to form an interdependent system. One common thread is professional development, which enhances all six performance areas. Improvement in one area generally leads to improvement in the others.

LPS for Leadership Evaluation

The LPS integrates three critical elements: goals, results, and learning. As Figure 1.2 and the ISLLC standards illustrate, these critical elements overlap. The first critical element, administrator's goals and expectations for the year, may be represented in a school or district plan, assigned by a supervisor, required by compliance such as NCLB, or may be self-generated. The goals, a plan to implement those goals, benchmarks for monitoring the process, and determination of resources needed to achieve those goals provide a foundation for the collaboration—and learning—that is part of the LPS process.

The second critical element, results, is related to student learning, leadership learning, systems learning, and reform. Outcome data is benchmarked throughout the LPS process, and results are reported at the end of the school term. The data provide an opportunity to review classroom practices and teacher performance while assessing systemwide results. Ranging from test scores to attendance figures, student data indicate progress toward achieving goals and help determine future goals. LPS enables leaders to put acquired student and school data into context to see how the data support their goals and match up with desired results. The data also link leadership to the core function of the school system—that is, student learning. In addition to student data, leaders might use other result indicators such as effects of a new standards-based curriculum or observations of innovative instructional practices.

Outcome data inform a school leader of the level of effectiveness achieved and identify areas that require additional focus. Because outcome data identify both the needs of the school system and those of the school leader, LPS contributes to the entire leadership evaluation protocol or process.

The third critical element of leadership evaluation is professional learning. Here school leaders identify specific professional development interests in and needs for advancing their leadership effectiveness. Through LPS and its peer-coaching element, leaders focus on the purpose of their work, monitor results, and seek feedback through professional collaborations, highlighting the need for professional development in their work rather than in a workshop.

■ THE LPS PROCESS

The LPS process consists of four phases. These four phases guide the leader's professional journey through a process that begins with defining a purpose. It moves on to setting goals, continues by building a plan for action and collaboration, and culminates with an articulation of outcomes and identification of new steps. Each element embedded in the LPS facilitates school leaders in goal setting, learning, and reflection. (See Figure 1.3 for a brief overview of the process. See also Appendix A.)

Figure 1.3   LPS Process

Phases of the Leadership Performance System

Purpose and Function

Theory of Action • Leadership Attributes and Standards

Focus for Learning

Goals • Banner Question

Process and Structures for Collaboration

Professional Learning Community • Feedback and Collaborations

Planning • Engagement • Collecting Evidence

Outcomes for Action Planning and Reporting Results

Action Plan • Assess Results • Reflect on Learnings • Set New Goals

The LPS process includes defining the administrator's leadership role and identifying the skills and actions that promote the school community's achievement of its goals. Activities at each phase guide school leaders in directing their inquiries as they collect evidence of their learning and acquire new understanding through collegial collaborations, which enable them to reflect on the effectiveness of their leadership on improving school culture.

The core function of a school system is to enhance and serve the student as learner. All actions and decisions should support student achievement. LPS provides school leaders with guidance, collaboration, and checkpoints to serve that core function. It informs school leaders of areas for growth and learning in response to the school system's needs. That focus results in improved learning outcomes for students.

The four phases of the LPS process are the following:

1. Purpose and function for work

2. Focus for learning

3. Process and structures for collaboration

4. Outcomes for action planning and reporting results

Phase One: Purpose and Function for Work

Establishing a purpose involves declaring and refining one's *theory of action*, commitment, and expectations for professional work. Defining one's theory of action provides a basis for meaningful work. Putting it in writing reminds school leaders of their commitment to and passion for what they do. In the course of work each day, a majority of the decisions they make stem from their theory of action, beliefs, and commitment. A clear understanding of what those are builds the foundation for decision making and gives them a yardstick for determining progress and a focus for collaboration and planning.

Also in this phase, LPS participants convene as a professional community to determine the characteristics of an effective leader, to review the ISLLC standards, and to establish the scope of leadership work. This process helps them acquire a more profound wisdom and an enriched perspective about their work as a community of educational leaders who seek alignment and shared understandings.

> LPS integrated the critical elements of an administrator's evaluation.

If the district requires LPS as a means of formal evaluation of school leaders, the benchmarking to standards and performance goals becomes a valuable tool that aligns with professional learning and collaborations in the school system. As a robust leadership performance evaluation process, the LPS provides a vehicle through which a school district may choose to integrate or insert its specific and unique evaluation requirements.

Phase Two: Focus for Learning

In phase two, school leaders determine the focus of their LPS and set their goals for the school and their own professional development. They establish an essential question (a *banner question*) that guides their learning and, subsequently, their leadership work.

LPS provides both a structure and a process that ideally aligns the professional development goals of the educational leader to school and district goals. The structure is the organization of LPS, including the four-phase design, tools, and worksheets, which help leaders focus on what they want to accomplish, where they want to grow, what goals they need to focus on, and results. The process includes the "softer" tools of collaboration, peer coaching, discussion, and reflection.

> LPS is both a structure and a process for aligning the school leader's goals with those of the district and school board.

The school board has specific goals and expectations for the district. As they set their LPS plan, educational leaders need to clarify alignment (agreement) between their plans and goals and that which the school board requires of them. Because district goals are usually broadly written, school leaders have some latitude.

Phase Three: Process and Structures for Collaboration

A performance action plan represents the leader's goals and priorities. The action planning process is constructed by combining schoolwide goals and priorities, generated with the staff, as a shared purpose and focus for action at the school site. These priorities, aligned with the school leader's performance goals, are integrated into the performance action planning. For example, if a schoolwide priority is to accelerate student performance in math and reading, the staff will work in grade-level teams to develop a plan for achieving that goal, and the school leader will align site-level work with his or her own goal to improve the school's AYP (annual yearly progress). Such an action plan includes a benchmarking process that helps to monitor progress, as well as tools that facilitate and engage the staff in planning, research, and implementation for school improvement.

> Participating in the LPS process with peers heightens the learning experience because peers offer knowledgeable contributions, observations, and feedback.

Structures for Collaboration

Participating in LPS with colleagues heightens the learning experience. Peer collaborations offer feedback, observations, and knowledge sharing, which inform decision making. In school systems that have implemented LPS, school leaders meet at a roundtable discussion group or other existing professional structures such as a principal meeting or a cabinet session. Periodically during the year, school leaders meet in a scheduled professional structure to review progress with their goals, professional learning, and action planning. They also may meet informally with an LPS partner.

An LPS partner is a peer of choice with whom the leader meets informally throughout the LPS process to discuss specific LPS activities and to consider other challenges and events that emerge during the course of work. Partners provide coaching and support to each other.

Meeting with a roundtable group is more structured and occurs four to six times during the year (the LPS cycle). Lasting about an hour or so, these meetings are opportunities for participants—two to four sets of LPS partners or four to eight participants total—to go around the table and review their progress and share next steps. These sessions are valuable because they expose the participants to a variety of viewpoints. Some school teams meet monthly; others meet every two weeks once they realize how valuable the process is in their daily work.

Meeting as a group allows participants the time and structure to discuss challenges, needs, and achievements. The most valuable—and powerful—benefit is the team effort and the emergence of ideas that might not have surfaced without the focused time together. Instead of meeting and talking about isolated events, the roundtable group focuses on specific targets and needs in the context of their LPS purpose and goals, which allows for rich conversation, not just retellings of events and concerns.

The collaboration in this phase of the LPS process also builds a professional community whose members all have the expectation of problem solving, learning, and improving one's work. In this phase, school leaders participate in the professional development activities they identified in the focus phase and begin collecting evidence and lessons learned as they progress toward meeting their professional and school goals.

Phase Four: Outcomes for Action Planning and Reporting Results

In this fourth and final phase of the LPS process, school leaders assess the evidence and results of their efforts. In particular, they examine their progress toward achieving the goals, a school administrator will also include progress with their school plan, improving school and student performance, and participating in professional development opportunities that contribute to their knowledge and effectiveness as school leaders.

This is also a time for them to reflect on the LPS process and share their insights and learning with peers in a roundtable session. Based on their feedback, they may adjust their action planning process undertaking, set new goals, and establish a new banner question.

THE BENEFITS OF LPS ■

The LPS provides a structure and process for reflection, collaboration, and learning. Its multidimensional performance process allows for contextual learning and a variety of sources for feedback. The LPS purpose and goals provide direction for the participant and create the arena and topics for exploration. Most importantly, LPS has the potential to facilitate the school leader's learning, allowing him or her to focus and construct their meaning of work and to measure progress. LPS increases collaboration, invites peer observation, and encourages community learning. It can be viewed as a container or organizer for the conversations, reflections, and inquiries about work.

As Figure 1.4 shows, the LPS process leaders do the following:

- *Focus professional and personal growth.* It identifies a target area for learning. Leaders select an area of concern or interest or one in which they need additional expertise and then articulate it in the form of a banner question.
- *Create and adapt personal learning plans.* It helps leaders select activities that contribute to their learning (inquiry) process, provide a variety of experiences, and highlight interactions with individuals and ideas.
- *Collect evidence and lessons learned.* As part of the process, leaders gather items that represent growth and reflect new understandings in the context of the banner question.
- *Monitor progress.* LPS assists in aligning performance goals and action plan priorities specific to the school leader's domain of responsibility.
- *Collaborate with peers one-on-one and in groups.* Leaders meet with an LPS partner or supervisor on an ongoing basis and in roundtable discussion groups with peers. Because groups may include colleagues with similar and different learning priorities, the opportunities for peer coaching and varied feedback are great.
- *Sharpen management skills.* Colleagues help each other identify management skills that get the job done. Leaders incorporate the skills into the banner question and, subsequently, into their professional development needs.
- *Apply leadership skills.* LPS participants identify characteristics of effective leaders and incorporate these characteristics into the banner question and professional development requirements.
- *Draw on past knowledge and experiences.* When forming the banner question and creating learning plans, leaders consider prior learning and use it as a starting point for inquiry.
- *Observe and contribute to collegial development.* LPS creates an environment in which every leader is a learner. Through collaboration with peers, participants act as both learners and leaders.
- *Assess the impact and influence of school district systems.* The process asks leaders to consider systems within the school and the district that support or interfere with outcomes related to the banner question.
- *Reflect on values, attitudes, and experiences.* School leaders collaborate with peers, write in their journals, collect data and evidence, reflect on learning activities, and have frequent and varied opportunities to consider colleagues' and their own points of view.

Figure 1.4 Benefits of the LPS

Benefits of the Leadership Performance System

- Focusing professional performance and learning

- Creating and adapting personal performance plans

- Collecting evidence of success

- Monitoring progress

- Collaborating with peers one-on-one and in groups

- Sharpening management skills

- Applying leadership skills

- Drawing on past knowledge and experiences

- Observing and contributing to collegial development

- Assessing the impact and influence of the school district systems

- Reflecting on one's performance, values, attitudes, and experiences

While the LPS can play a role in a school system's evaluation process, it also can contribute to a leader's self-evaluation. Collegial collaborations can lead participants to recognize their own strengths and challenges. This self-awareness produces a greater likelihood that they will engage in learning opportunities in an effort to grow. The feedback provided in a trusting and respectful environment of a roundtable discussion or one-on-one meeting with a performance LPS partner assists leaders in identifying areas that will improve their effectiveness.

THE IMPORTANCE OF LEADERS AS LEARNERS

No one can mandate leaders to be learners. However, the leadership community can make a conscious decision to build a professional learning community, thus shaping its work and design to meet a shared purpose.

Lifelong learning is a demand of the information era. Knowledge is temporary, and everyone must be able to continually adapt and learn at a pace outside one's comfort range. Lifelong learning is the ability to continually enhance, modify, and restructure one's understanding by interacting with other people, ideas, and situations. These new understandings lead to new practices and models for learning and evaluation within the school system.

Educational leaders should experience and be able to model this ability as part of their leadership role in a school system. Thus, the role of educational leader demands attributes of *knowledge leadership*. A knowledge leader has the ability to facilitate the transformation of data and information into knowledge, the capacity to apply new understandings to actual practice. A knowledge leader establishes professional structures and learning communities where participants continually inform and refine the system as they identify priorities, needs, and resources that are timely, relevant, and actionable (Dietz, Barker, & Giberson, 2005).

LPS provides the structure and process for educational leaders to perform as knowledge leaders. As they engage with colleagues, they expand their capacity and leadership repertoire. At the same time, they model the process for students and other community members. Through reflections and by continually incorporating new ideas into practice, they actually establish the attributes of a learning organization. The LPS process provides an envelope for the mind that provides both a framework and a context for the learner.

In each phase of LPS (Figure 1.5), participants must ask themselves a series of questions related to their professional goals and the goals of the school community they serve. As they progress, they take with them the knowledge and insights acquired in the previous phases. After they have completed the final phase and have assessed the outcomes, they must set new goals for growth and learning.

Figure 1.5   The School Leader's Progress Through the Four Phases of the LPS Process

Purpose and Role of Leadership

- Describe professional theory of action
- Define leadership performance and standards

Focus for Learning

- Focus for LPS in the school system
- Focus the leader's LPS theme and set goals through creation of a banner question—an essential question that will drive inquiry and learning for the current year

Process and Structures for Collaboration

- Meet with colleagues one-on-one and in roundtable group sessions
- Identify structures/groups already in place that can support your LPS
- Create performance plans
- Participate in professional development activities
- Collect evidence

Outcomes for Action Planning and Reporting Results

- Reflect on progress, share learning, and set new goals.

GETTING READY TO DESIGN   ■
AND IMPLEMENT YOUR LPS

When I first began to work with school systems in designing and implementing a leadership portfolio process, I faced great resistance. The overall response was, "We are too busy doing our work. We do not have time to DO a portfolio." Administrators were so distracted with the demands of mandates, legal challenges, test scores, and the ongoing list of day-to-day demands, not to mention the school board and community's vigilant watching, they could not take the time to make what they perceived was a scrapbook. However, some clusters of administrators I worked with truly tried to find the time, space, and energy to participate. They found themselves in the minority and eventually wanted to join the club of "I don't have the time." I was concerned, frustrated, but still eager to explore the possibilities of helping them clearly define their purpose for the portfolio and then design a process that would facilitate the process as a community of learners.

That was it! All of a sudden it dawned on me that while the portfolio might have been perceived as busywork, the notion of leaders taking the time for their own learning and development was just not a norm in their system. I thought of my own journey as an educational leader and the role of learning in my work as well as how I was fitting it in my professional life. Then the pieces started coming together.

First, if learning is essential for continuous improvement in education, then leaders must be learners. Second, the leadership role is so burdened with tactical and strategic planning and action that time for learning, reflection, and collaboration is sorely overlooked. Last, but not least, the practice of a professional community working and learning together is a missing link. By design, there are more competitive cultural norms than collaborative norms for educational leaders. However, if the portfolio process had proved to be so successful for teacher development and as a vehicle for building capacity in schools, could that portfolio process be redesigned to offer similar enhancements to the work of administrators?

These reflections led to development of a portfolio design and process to assist the work of educational leaders. The portfolio process

- builds a professional learning community,
- creates the space for reflections and collaboration, and
- accomplishes this in the context of goal setting and achievement toward meeting professional, site, and districtwide goals.

The portfolio has become a vehicle to move through the goal-oriented, tactical, and strategic work of educational leaders while it has built capacity in new areas, solidified learning from experiences, and built a professional community with collaboration and support for success.

Educational leaders are eager to have such a learning community in which to learn and grow. Currently, many school systems do not provide the opportunities for administrative professional growth. Using the portfolio process as an entry point for responding to this critical need, the work of leadership and the power of collaboration, reflection, and learning have led to systemic changes in school systems. The portfolio process, once designed, implemented, and nurtured, provides a change that continues to add value to educational systems.

■ LPS PORTFOLIO

LPS can be captured in any form participants wish it to take. It can be a three-ring binder, a journal, a computer file, or a DVD. Accompanying the discussion of each phase of the process are worksheets and tools that school leaders can use as general organizers or journal entries. Leaders complete the information, evidence, and other materials according to their preferences and needs, unless the district prescribes a specific compilation technique for evaluation purposes.

2

Establishing a Purpose for the LPS

THE FIRST PHASE OF THE LPS ■

Establishing the purpose for the LPS is the first of the four phases of the LPS process. In this phase, participants begin building a professional community, define their professional theory of action, and determine a shared purpose such as professional development, credentialing, evaluation, and school improvement planning for participating in the process. Participants also determine how the LPS will align with their work and with their school system.

Note that participants do not leave one phase behind when they enter the next. The process requires them to refer continually to the earlier phases, with each phase building on the previous phase. While they need to complete some activities in the process only once, others are ongoing throughout the process and throughout their professional careers. Figure 2.1 outlines the steps and the corresponding phase of the LPS. (A template of Figure 2.1 appears in Appendix B.)

Figure 2.1

Steps in the LPS Process

The first three steps of the LPS process mark the school leader's introduction to the process and set the stage for the remainder of the process. Steps four through seven define ongoing activities, which take place throughout the LPS process.

Introduction to the LPS Process

Step 1: Participate in the initial purpose-setting session (phase one).

Step 2: Focus LPS by identifying goals and establishing banner question (phase two).

Step 3: Identify professional structures for collaborations and an LPS partner and a collaboration network, and begin process of collaboration and activities (phase three).

Ongoing Activities Within the LPS Process

Step 4: Set school/district and school administrator's professional development goals, establish learning plans, and collect artifacts and evidence (phases two and three).

Step 5: Design the Action Plan (phase four).

Step 6: Engage in roundtable sessions (phases one, two, three, and four).

Step 7: Evaluate outcomes and determine effectiveness of the process; make adaptations as indicated (phase four).

◼ ESTABLISHING A PURPOSE FOR THE LPS

The process starts with the community of leaders coming together to define their purpose and expectations for engaging in the LPS. This community might be composed of school leaders who have come together on their own or a group of administrators that has been convened by the school or district superintendent or director. Whether the LPS is used as part of a formal leadership evaluation or as the means of directing and assessing one's own work, participants need to define the standards and expectations for school leaders and outcomes for engagement in the process.

◼ LEADERSHIP STANDARDS AND EXPECTATIONS

Those embarking on the process must first explore definitions of leadership to focus and monitor their leadership development and overall effectiveness. This task also helps them clarify the purpose and function of the LPS. Participants should also consider school policy or statewide mandates related to leadership standards and expectations of performance. A shared set of leadership standards helps participants determine areas of focus for professional development.

P. David Pearson (1993) pointed out the importance of beginning any discussion of standards by defining the purpose and function of standards. Standards serve the following functions:

- *Direct momentum.* Standards provide a target and act as milestones, which provide guidance en route to that target.
- *Indicate performance.* Standards act as a yardstick that measures and defines progress.
- *Clarify transactions, responsibilities, and rights.* Standards set boundaries for the accountability, function, and role of the standards in the learning and assessment cycle including who will use the standards and how will they use them.

Whatever leadership standard the community of leaders constructs or adopts, the conversation and agreement on critical areas for growth is an important beginning point in the process. To clarify their roles and their definitions of standards and leadership, the group might discuss the following questions (see also Figure 2.2):

- How do we define the role and function of leadership in our system?
- What standards and guidelines do we wish to employ to create common understanding and common expectations of what we strive for in our ongoing leadership development?
- What state, organizational, or national standards might assist in determining our assessments and expectations?
- How will we align the LPS with our district administrator evaluation?

Figure 2.2

Sample Standards for School Leaders

The Interstate School Leaders Licensure Consortium (ISLLC; 1996) has developed the following standards for school administrators:

Educational leaders promote the success of all students by

1. facilitating the development, articulation, implementation, and stewardship of a vision of learning that is shared and supported by the school community;

2. advocating, nurturing, and sustaining a school culture and instructional program conducive to student learning and staff professional growth;

3. ensuring management of the organization, operations, and resources for a safe, efficient, and effective learning environment;

4. collaborating with families and community members, responding to diverse community interests and needs, and mobilizing community resources;

5. acting with integrity and fairness and in an ethical manner;

6. understanding, responding to, and influencing the larger political, social, economic, legal, and cultural contexts.

For more information on the work of ISLLC, visit their Web site at http://www.ccsso.org/standards.html.

In the LPS context, standards can provide guidelines for participants' discussions about capacity building. As leaders begin customizing the LPS to their local needs, the leadership standards and expectations can serve as organizers for reflection and for conversations about performance data and evaluation. Of course, tying standards into the LPS is vital to evaluation, whether self-assessment or a formal evaluation process. Evaluation of the work of educational leaders addresses the areas of performance, feedback, decisions, and standards, so during the process, leaders should ask themselves questions such as the following:

> Participants must have a shared set of standards to focus their efforts.

- *Performance.* How am I performing in the context of generating a shared purpose and goals for the school community? How much progress am I making toward those goals? How am I monitoring my progress?
- *Feedback.* How can I get feedback from my work and from my peers to improve my performance?
- *Decisions.* How am I making decisions, and how am I assessing their impact on the school system?
- *Standards.* What are the district's expectations of my work? What are the school community's expectations, including staff, students, and parents? How do we, as a leadership community, define the standards for our work? What are the critical attributes and capacities of a high-performing administrator?

One school district that has implemented the LPS has established the following eight areas of performance for administrators:

- Participate with teacher and parent groups to provide leadership
- Support student growth and development
- Foster a positive school climate
- Honor diversity and promote equity of opportunity
- Stimulate, focus, and support improvement of instruction
- Manage administrative, fiscal, and facilities functions
- Foster effective district team relationships
- Promote professional development of school personnel

Using the ISLLC standards, presented in Chapter 1, provides a framework for evaluating the effectiveness of administrators. As Figure 2.3 indicates, tangible behaviors and a clearly defined process help guide the evaluation in concrete ways.

Figure 2.3

ISLLC Standards and LPS in Alignment

(Used with permission)

ISLLC STANDARD	LEADERSHIP PERFORMANCE SYSTEM
Standard 1 A school administrator is an educational leader who promotes the success of all students by **facilitating the development, articulation, implementation, and stewardship of a vision** of learning that is shared and supported by the school community.	**PURPOSE** Leadership reflection of values, beliefs, and commitment–*Credo* **FOCUS** Priorities for action and for professional learning Employ systems planning model Use communication conventions
Standard 2 A school administrator is an educational leader who promotes the success of all students by **advocating, nurturing, and sustaining a school culture and instructional program** conducive to student learning and staff professional growth.	**PURPOSE** Alignment of vision, mission, and goals **PROCESS/STRUCTURES** Culture assessments, for reform readiness Review and establish professional learning community Relationships–roles and responsibilities Professional development for job-embedded learning Establish performance and professional learning goals
Standard 3 A school administrator is an educational leader who promotes the success of all students by ensuring management of the **organization, operations, and resources for a safe, efficient, an effective learning environment**.	**FOCUS/STRUCTURES** Alignment of goals and performance standards, identification of professional learning structure for completing work such as board, district leadership, leadership roundtable **PROCESS** Monitoring progress and making adaptations in planning as indicated **OUTCOMES** Determine action priorities Establish decision-making processes and communication conventions Practices to promote a theory of action
Standard 4 A school administrator is an educational leader who promotes the success for all students by **collaborating with families and community members, responding to diverse community interests, and needs, and mobilizing community resources**.	**PROCESS** Establish committees, focus groups, and parent advisories, identification of professional learning structure for completing the work such as school site council, parent groups, business/leadership roundtable Use meeting conventions and sustain active communications **OUTCOMES** Outreach to stakeholders, community, and board Engagement in action priorities

Figure 2.3   Continued

ISLLC STANDARD	LEADERSHIP PERFORMANCE SYSTEM
Standard 5 A school administrator is an educational leader who promotes the success of all students by **acting with integrity, fairness, an in an ethical manner.**	**PURPOSE** Clear purpose of the role of educational leadership in their community Commitment to honor shared and diverse values of the school community and the community at large **PROCESS** Employ professional efficacy and ethical frameworks to lead by example with exemplar ethical behaviors for the educational community
Standard 6 A school administrator is an educational leader who promotes the success for all students by **understanding, responding to, and influencing the larger political, social, economic, legal, and cultural context**.	**PURPOSE** Communicate vision and mission **PROCESS/STRUCTURES** Sustain outreach structures for convening the stakeholder group/identification of professional learning structure for completing the work—that is, board, district leadership, local government/leadership roundtable Establish a sustainable communication process with stakeholders **OUTCOMES** Professional network and learning community System planning procedures Report results and plan for continuous improvement Integrate new learning and feedback into practice

DEFINING THE LPS PURPOSE AND FUNCTION ■

Defining leadership standards and the LPS purpose can take place at the first roundtable session among participants. To prepare for the meeting and the discussion about purpose, participants should be sure that they have a clear understanding of the purpose and function of the LPS in the context of district expectations. If the district requires the participation as part of its formal evaluation of school leaders, the major preparation is aligning the LPS with the district's existing plans and expectations. All parties must agree on the purpose of the LPS and establish their expectations in advance of the project.

While determining the purpose of the LPS as part of the district's formal evaluation or as a leadership development system, participants should share their perceptions of the LPS by completing the Agreement on Purpose tool. Roundtable members then come to an agreement on how they will use the process and support each other.

Agreement on Purpose Tool

The Agreement on Purpose tool is important because having alignment regarding the purpose and desired outcome of participation in the LPS is a critical starting point for participants. Being aligned on purpose provides the group members with a context for decision making within the LPS, a yardstick to measure progress toward goals, a list of priorities for action related to the goals and the banner question, and a focus for collaboration with other participants. As each step in the process requires decisions, leaders who are clear on their purpose will be better informed to make decisions on what to focus, on what evidence and data to collect, and so forth.

The Agreement on Purpose tool consists of three statements. The first statement involves individual perspective of the purpose of the LPS. The second statement asks participants to identify how they believe work with their peers and their participation in professional learning activities can improve their work. The third statement calls for them to identify three anticipated outcomes of their participation in the process.

> Aligning the purpose and desired outcome of the LPS provides a context for decision making.

Follow these steps for completing the tool as a group:

1. Participants take seven to ten minutes to reflect on the statements and write their responses. This time for individual reflection and response before a group discussion gives each participant a chance to articulate a response and thus promotes sharing of individual wisdom.

2. When participants finish their responses, they divide into groups of three to five, share their reflections and their responses to the first question of purpose, and then create a group response to the question.

3. Each group shares its responses, and when the entire group has a collective mind-set of purpose, the group crafts a shared purpose statement.

4. The small groups discuss each member's response to the second statement, which helps each individual recognize the value of working together and of lifelong learning.

5. The small groups share each member's response to the third statement related to outcomes, then share the responses of the small group with the whole group. The entire group creates a master list of desired outcomes that all can see on a chart or chalkboard, eliminating redundancies and combining similar outcomes until the group has a list of about seven to twelve outcomes for the LPS.

6. The participants next prioritize the outcomes by means of a "magic marker vote." They review the outcomes and vote for priorities. Each person makes three marks on the master list to indicate his or her priorities; the person can place all three marks on one outcome or disperse them among two or three outcomes. This technique provides an accounting of the group's goals and builds the foundation for effective design and implementation of the LPS.

An example of an agreement on purpose tool appears in Figure 2.4, and Figure 2.5 presents a completed agreement on purpose tool. (For your convenience, both items also appear and in the appendices at the end of the book.)

Figure 2.4

Agreement on Purpose

From my point of view, the primary purpose of the LPS is as follows:

Collaboration and learning can enhance my work in the following ways:

I will consider my time and efforts with the LPS worthwhile if the following events occur:

Figure 2.5

Sample Agreement on Purpose

From my point of view, the primary purpose of the LPS is as follows:

The purpose is to provide a structure and process for me and my colleagues to talk about our work. I would welcome an opportunity to have constructive feedback and, most of all, suggestions for working more effectively and efficiently. Another purpose that would serve my work would be to create an environment where we have less competition and more collaboration. The LPS can also serve as a documentation of my work and learning.

Collaboration and learning can enhance my work in the following ways:

I would like to know more about the work of others in our school system. I seem to be informed many times after the fact. Such collaboration can offer feedback and possibly more timely flow of information. I would benefit from sharing in efforts and past experiences of others in the school system. The challenge for us is to establish an environment for collaboration—one we have not always had in the past.

I will consider my time and efforts with the LPS worthwhile if the following events occur:

1. *We integrate the process into our current leadership meetings and assessment process.*

2. *We produce documents worthy of sharing when applying for future employment.*

3. *We build a collaboration network among leaders in our system.*

■ DEFINING ONE'S THEORY OF ACTION

The theory of action is rooted in a sociotechnical system that helps explain how we begin to envision just how our current state can be rearranged to result in a change. In practice, the theory of action is an explanation of what we are currently doing, why we are doing it, and a mental map by which to make decisions in the course of moving forward with our work.

In defining a theory of action, consider the synthesis of ideas, research, and the study of one's experiences, focused on action for a desired result. The key elements to consider when constructing a theory of action around specific goals, and the questions to ask, include the following:

- If student achievement is one of your goals, what are the best steps and top priorities to lead the action?
- What has research and your experiences taught you about what works and what does not?
- What is the current state of research regarding instruction?
- What is the readiness level for change and the current level of use regarding the teacher's repertoire for powerful instruction?
- What success models will help you as you prepare for action?
- What are the essential environmental changes necessary to truly inform the action planning process in your school system?

School leaders need to reflect on their knowledge, beliefs, attitudes, and values about education and leadership in general and their own work in particular. While every education program asks educators to define their philosophy (and theory of action), sometimes this philosophy becomes buried beneath bureaucratic demands. This step of the LPS invites leaders to reflect once again on their philosophy and how it is expressed in their theory of action and place them in the forefront as a significant influence on every aspect of their work.

Participants should complete the Defining Your Theory of Action tool (a template follows in Figure 2.6 and appears in Appendix C). LPS partners then share and compare their philosophies. Doing so sets the foundation for their work together. It allows them to see why they do what they do—what beliefs and knowledge provide the underpinnings of their work. An example of how one school leader completed the Defining Your Theory of Action tool appears in Figure 2.7. The completed sample (Figure 2.7) also appears in Appendix D.

Figure 2.6

Defining Your Theory of Action

Take this opportunity to reflect on your Theory of Action, and then share your perspectives with a partner or member of your roundtable.

What beliefs do you hold about the purpose and function of leadership?

Describe your perspective of a most effective management system or routine.

What beliefs do you hold about how people learn?

What are your top three priorities in your work?

Figure 2.7

Sample Defining Your Theory of Action

Take this opportunity to reflect on your Theory of Action, and then share your perspectives with a partner or member of your roundtable.

What beliefs do you hold about the purpose and function of leadership?

The purpose of leadership is to create an environment for collaboration, commitment, and learning among the professionals and other staff members in the school system. Leaders do not have all the answers; they must develop, nurture, and draw on the expertise and wisdom of all members in the system.

Describe your perspective of a most effective management system or routine.

This is not my greatest area of strength. I have found setting goals annually is very important. When I have been disciplined enough to set goals for my work, I have been able to establish work plans to correspond with checkpoints, and the technique does seem to work. The challenge to this system is not overlooking the first step—focus and plan. Then the rest of the tactical aspects of the job seem to follow along.

What beliefs do you hold about how people learn?

I believe we learn in a very natural way, using experimentation and new information as well as prior experiences to try new things. It is through those interactions that we construct new understandings and expand our repertoire of knowledge. The information we take in to solve problems and meet new challenges adds to our knowledge and repertoire of understanding. Thus, it is a continuous process.

What are your top three priorities in your work?

My priorities are to build commitment and capacity among staff members, to offer a learner-centered instructional program, and to listen to community and other professional input regarding research, innovations, and global needs to prepare students for the future. As educators, we must first do no harm.

SUMMARY OF LPS CONTENTS   ■

At the end of the first phase of the process, the LPS contains the following materials:

From Phase One—Purpose and Function for Work

- Written definition of leadership standards, attributes, and expectations
- Agreement on Purpose
- Defining Your Theory of Action

With these materials in hand, participants are ready to move on to the second phase of the process, establishing its focus by identifying professional goals and creating a banner question.

3

Focusing the LPS

THE CONVERGENCE OF GOALS ■
AND PROFESSIONAL DEVELOPMENT

In the first phase of the LPS, school leaders establish a purpose for the LPS and define their theory of action for leadership. The community of learners discusses standards, attributes, and expectations for leadership performance in their professional setting.

In the second phase, school leaders determine the focus of their LPS. They begin by establishing connections among their work, performance goals, and professional needs. Looking at their performance goals and challenges, school plan, and district expectations, school leaders search for alignments among their goals. These alignments help to define a theme(s) in regard to their professional learning, and planning for action—this theme becomes the focus of their LPS. As part of their professional development, they reflect on their personal interests and talents, as well as on their needs for learning, exploration, and accountability. A leader's ultimate challenge is to be true to one's self, one's moral purpose for doing the work, one's commitment to achieving results, and to build capacity among one's educational community to sustain results.

The leader's challenge and imperative is to find a constructive method of melding internal and external needs and demands without conflict. When there is a lack of alignment among values, beliefs, and attitudes and doing the job, the leader and the school system ultimately do not benefit. Leaders make decisions many times during the day. These decisions are informed by their learning and surrounded by their beliefs, values, and attitudes toward others and their work. When in the heat of making an important and urgent decision, we often fall back on our beliefs, values, and attitudes. This has been proven through observing leaders engaged in the LPS. Discussion and reflections regarding core beliefs, values, and attitudes brings to the forefront discussion and alignment with a leader's professional work. In some cases, they even inform the leader that they might not be in the right time and place to do the work. In either case, the LPS process offers a venue to include this critical attribute that influences a leader's theory of action.

In one high school district, a building principal was convinced that the students did not care and that engagement and personalization had no place in their high-poverty, at-risk high school. He was making this decision based on observable attitudes of the students—how they did not take school seriously and that the teachers were working hard delivering their content; they were doing their best with what they had to work with. As part of his participation in the LPS, he articulated this in his writing and goals setting. During a discussion with other participants, they began to explore, discuss, and debate some of the root causes for failure and where to begin. One of the leadership roundtable members shared Martin Habermin's "Pedagogy of Poverty." His research highlights the key attributes of instructional practices in most high-poverty schools. This discussion extended into an ongoing debate and study, which led to actual observations to determine if, in fact, student lack of engagement and current instructional practices might be contributing to, rather than solving, the problem of student apathy and low performance results. As you might assume, this did become the leader's LPS focus for learning and goal setting, as well as for providing an influence on other participants to consider the same essential question: "How can we improve student engagement in our high school?"

This process of searching for areas where goals, school plans, and professional learning intersect brings meaning to leaders' work and relevance to their learning.

■ DETERMINING GOALS IN THE LPS

In most cases, school leaders determine their performance goals in concert with the school board and the superintendent or supervisor's direction, with input from school faculty and community members. These goals then become the driving force for action planning. Goals are usually influenced by federal and state mandates, as well as by community needs, and they have long- and short-term expectations. An example of a district's mission statement and goals appears in the following paragraph and demonstrates how district goals, as defined by the district's mission statement, set the direction for the goals of the educational leader and thus, the LPS.

The mission is to close the achievement gap; District X is committed to providing opportunities for *all* students to

- participate as responsible and informed citizens in a safe and healthy environment;
- use technology as a tool for communicating, learning, and working;

- acquire knowledge and skills to ensure successful and fulfilling career paths;
- engage in a rigorous academic environment with relevant learning;
- develop self-esteem and respect for self and others;
- become lifelong learners who communicate effectively, think critically, and solve problems in a team environment.

> Goals for the LPS should reflect federal, state, and community requirements and influences.

School leaders can take the district mission statement and translate it into their leadership goals. For example, based on the preceding mission statement, the board of education established these goals:

- All students will read, write, and calculate at their appropriate grade level according to the standards set by the state.
- Develop a revised curriculum that aligns the standards with multiple sources of student data to demonstrate learning.
- Inform parents and community members of the standards and new assessments to monitor learning.
- Design a new process for reporting student progress that aligns with the standards and assessments.
- Enhance professional development opportunities that include application of learning and peer coaching.
- Refine the administrator evaluation system.

When school leaders develop their school plan, they engage their staff in a purpose and priority-setting activity. Seeking a shared set of priorities can focus action planning for the year. Leaders also ask themselves questions such as the following: What mandates and unique needs am I facing this year? What does our school data tell us about our current state? What do we need to do as a school community to build our capacity to accelerate learning for all students? The plan should include professional learning opportunities and success indicators. Leaders can examine these indicators or benchmarks at predetermined checkpoints during the term to monitor the plan's progress.

THE FOCUSED LEADER ■

The Venn diagram in Figure 3.1 serves as a visual organizer of focused leadership. (A copy of the diagram also appears in Appendix C.) School leaders can use the diagram to list professional development goals along with leadership responsibilities for the year. The three areas of inquiry and development are separate yet integrated:

- *School plan.* The school plan combines the needs of the specific site and its students with the district goals and expectations. The school plan should include the essentials listed in the preceding section.

- *Goals.* As stated previously, the goals become the driving force for action planning. In addition to district goals, school leaders should list goals unique to their school and student's, as well as their own individual goals for professional growth.
- *Professional learning.* School leaders should consider professional requirements, but should also consider their own interests, asking themselves the following questions:

  (a)   What do I want to learn more about?

  (b)   What knowledge and skills do I want to develop?

  (c)   What professional relationships do I want to enhance?

The graphic organizer helps school leaders see and discuss with their peers any overlap and determine ways to capitalize on any redundancies, integrating their learning and their work. Then, when setting professional development goals or identifying professional development activities within the LPS, they can focus on a few specific topics that appear in the three areas of their work and professional needs.

Figure 3.1

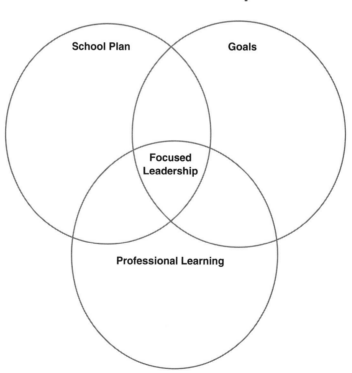

Focused Leadership

School Plan

Goals

Focused Leadership

Professional Learning

INVOLVING SCHOOL STAFF ■

The next step in the process is involving staff members in the priority- and goal-setting process as a learning community. Engaging staff who report to the school leader directly in the LPS process by aligning their goals and priorities with those of the school leader helps the leader accomplish his or her goals.

The first step in including staff members in the process is having them meet and together complete Establishing Targeted Priority Goals (Figure 3.2). Establishing Targeted Priority Goals involves the staff in the goal-setting process for their school plan and targets priority goals for professional learning. Establishing Targeted

> Engaging staff in the LPS process helps school leaders accomplish their goals.

Priority Goals and folding the staff goals into the school plan gives school leaders a focus for their professional work and learning and a context for collaborations with their colleagues.

The steps for completing Establishing Targeted Priority Goals mirrors the facilitation process Agreement on Purpose described in Chapter 2. Bring staff together and introduce the tool, which consists of four statements. (See the following template in Figure 3.2. Another copy of the template appears in Appendix C and is provided in the LPS CD.) The first statement involves the individual perspective identifying the focus and priority goal for their professional work this year. The second statement relates to commitment and competency, and it asks participants to identify the skills, knowledge, and expertise and level of commitment to their work. The third and fourth statements have staff specify strategies, skills, and expertise they need to expand to be successful with implementing targeted priority goals and to establish benchmarks for checkpoints to monitor progress.

Follow these steps for introducing the Establishing Targeted Priority Goals worksheet:

1. Explain the purpose for identifying shared goals for the term. Describe the power of Establishing Targeted Priority Goals: It ensures that everyone aims in the same direction and agrees on the purpose and the process for the shared journey. It also gives a shared context for decision making, a yardstick to measure progress, and a focus for collaboration and action planning.

2. Invite staff members to reflect on the statements and allow them about seven to ten minutes to jot down their responses. (Background music invites quiet, individual reflection.) Explain the rationale for beginning with individual points of view. First, it helps avoid groupthink, where the first person to speak shares an opinion and the others agree, and rather than a sharing of individual wisdom, group agreement on one person's idea occurs. Second, staff members are better able to participate if they have had time to reflect and focus on the questions and formulate responses. They are more articulate and focused in their responses, having gone through a reflective composing process to distill their thinking.

3. When they finish their responses, place staff in groups of three to five. Have them share their reflections and their responses to the first question of their priority goals for the year. Have the small groups share their responses, and when the entire group has a collective mind-set shared priority goals, have them generate a list of priority goals they have in common. For example, they might have grade-level or department-specific instructional goals and a shared/common content area, strategy, or assessment target in common.

4. Prioritize the goals by means of a "magic marker vote." Invite staff members to review the goals and vote for priorities. Ask them each to make three marks on the master list to indicate their priorities; they can place all three marks on one goal or disperse them among two or three goals. This technique provides an accounting of the group's priorities. The statement of purpose and the list of goals in priority order provide school leaders with a foundation on which they can generate a school or work plan for the term.

5. After they have prioritized the top three to five priority goals for the year, as a staff, have them form action priority teams, each team assuming responsibility for one of the goals selected. The teams will check in with each other and the school leader periodically during the term. The check-in gives the leader a continual progress report and gives each action team a self-assessment on its progress toward achieving the goal.

6. Now meeting in their newly formed action priority teams have the teams discuss the second statement, which helps each individual recognize his or her own expertise in successfully achieving their priority goals for the year. As a team they can begin to share their collective knowledge and skills aimed at their priority goal and as they identify professional development needs for their work.

7. Have groups share their responses to the third statement related to essential benchmarks toward achieving their goals. Have the action priority teams establish their benchmarks and checkpoints to monitor progress with their action team priority goal and evidence of sustaining the gain at the end of the term. The teams will check in with each other and the school leader periodically during the term. The check-in gives the leader a continual progress report and gives each action team a self-assessment on its progress toward achieving the goal.

Figure 3.3 offers an example of one staff member's completed Establishing Targeted Priorities Goals. (The sample completed tool also appears in Appendix D.)

Figure 3.2

Establishing Targeted Priority Goals

The focus and priority goals for my professional work this year are as follows:

I currently have the following expertise and commitment to achieving these goals:

Specific strategies, skills, and expertise I would like to expand to be successful with implementing these instructional priorities are as follows:

Essential benchmarks for achievement toward my goals include the following:

Figure 3.3

Sample Establishing Targeted Priority Goals

The focus and priority goals for my professional work this year are as follows:

- *Implement standards-based instruction in mathematics*

- *Use data to determine the appropriate instructional level for students*

- *Plan differentiated instruction about identified student needs*

- *Establish intervention strategies and study groups for students who are having a difficult time meeting the grade-level standards.*

I currently have the following expertise and commitment to achieving these goals:

As a teacher, I have designed differentiation strategies, in mathematics for students in my class. I will support my colleagues in analyzing their student data to determine the student grouping and instructional strategies to support accelerated achievement in mathematics.

Specific strategies, skills, and expertise I would like to expand to be successful with implementing these instructional priorities are as follows:

I would like to have new formative assessments that we could use as a grade level team to monitor progress and inform our instructional planning in mathematics. I would also like to work with my grade level and mathematics team in determining their professional development needs to build an action plan around these priority goals targeted at student achievement.

Essential benchmarks for achievement toward my goals include the following:

I will with my team and look at student data to reach agreement in realistic benchmarks and scheduled checkpoints to update progress with the design, implementation, and progress with the goals.

The next step is for school leaders to reflect on and assess their work and to determine what challenges, needs, and opportunities might be on the horizon.

DETERMINING PERFORMANCE BENCHMARKS ■

The focused leader now has a set of clearly defined performance goals and school priority goals. Part of a performance action plan is establishing benchmarks for progress and expected results for the end of the year. The exact set of expectations is determined with the superintendent or other supervisory colleagues as the leader begins to align the action planning and monitoring progress process for the year. If the LPS is integrated with the leadership performance evaluation process in the district, the benchmark checkpoint process can be reviewed at roundtable sessions and during one-on-ones with the superintendent or supervisor.

IDENTIFYING SUCCESS INDICATORS ■

The work or school plan lists specific goals. The next step is to determine what indicators to use to assess progress toward meeting those goals. In the preceding example of designing a district wide professional development model for teachers and negotiating alternative assessment with the teacher's union, this school leader might assess current professional development activities, specifically, their effect on classroom instruction and areas for improvement. Indicators might be documentation of past practices and suggestions for improved planning. Establishing an open negotiation process with the union will accommodate research and input from both sides.

For the school leader who wishes to construct a standards-based curriculum, indicators might be establishing grade level teams and designing and implementing a process to help teachers understand the purpose and process for standards-based instruction at their grade level. These examples are benchmark indicators. They align with staff's establishment of priorities, which includes constructing an action plan and moving toward a shared, schoolwide goal. The benchmarks help identify success indicators and assess every step of the process of achieving the goals set out in the action plan and, thus, help leaders make appropriate adaptations in subsequent steps in the process.

ESTABLISHING A BANNER QUESTION ■

In phase two of the LPS process, school leaders establish a banner question for learning, collaborating, and reflecting. The purpose of the banner question is to focus learning and leadership capacity building. Leaders consider the dimensions of leadership involved in their inquiry, based on the ISLLC standards (see Appendix E), and they explore learning opportunities that will help them integrate these dimensions throughout their plan.

The focused leadership diagram that appears in this chapter (Figure 3.1) and Appendix C helps leaders look for connections among their work, their professional development, and their school plans. For example, under school plans, a school leader might write, "Create a three-year budget," under goals might write, "Learn to prepare budget," and under professional learning might write, "I will take a course in finance and network with a colleague who has created a similar budget." The Establishing Targeted Priority Goals worksheet the staff completed can facilitate the process of aligning staff goals with district and community goals. Leaders should use each of the worksheets in this book as tools for reflection, suggestions for action, and guidelines for identifying and organizing goals and tracking progress toward the goals. Most important, they help leaders focus on the key aspect of the LPS process: the banner question.

> The banner question is the essential question for inquiry and learning for the current year.

A reflection worksheet for formulating the banner question follows and also appears in Appendix C. The banner question is the essential question for inquiry and learning for the current year. The "Big Idea" question drives school leaders' work and inquiry. It helps leaders focus their work, their conversations, and their professional learning. This question might not represent the entirety of their work; however, it represents a primary theme. It is usually related to goals—both professional development goals and work goals. Formulating a banner question takes time, reflection, and collaborative conversations.

Splinter questions are the smaller steps that lead to constructing new understanding about work and professional learning.

When completing a Banner Question worksheet, LPS participants should respond to the following questions:

- What do I already know about [banner question topic]?
- What have I heard about or observed that especially interests me?
- What would I like to do differently?
- What are my wants and needs for my professional life?

As school leaders reflect on and respond to the questions, they bring their needs, concerns, and wisdom to the LPS process, defining the focus for their LPS work. The power of this personal reflection is magnified when they follow up individual reflections with conversations with their colleagues, either informally with an LPS partner or more formally in a roundtable session with colleagues in diverse leadership positions within the school system. A sample template and a completed Banner Question worksheet appear in Figures 3.4 and Figure 3.5. (Both also appear in the appendices.)

Figure 3.4   Banner Question

Banner Question

Write your banner question here; remember that you can refine the question later.

Splinter Questions

What additional questions do you need to answer before you can answer your banner question?

1.   What do I already know about [banner question topic]?

2.   What have I heard about or observed that especially interests me?

3.   What would I like to do differently?

4.   What are my wants and needs for my professional life?

Figure 3.5   Completed Banner Question

Banner Question

Write your banner question here; remember that you can refine the question later.

How can I use the mandate to design and implement standards-based curriculum with performance assessments as an opportunity to enhance and expand student learning?

Splinter Questions

What additional questions do you need to answer before you can answer your banner question?

- *What are successful models for performance assessments?*

- *What additional skills and training will staff members need to design a standards-based curriculum?*

- *What information and experience will they need to understand and use performance assessments?*

- *How will we modify our report card to reflect the new assessments and curriculum?*

- *To what degree will we need to modify our current instructional model?*

- *What new instruction materials will we need to make the curriculum shift?*

1. What do I already know about a standards-based curriculum and performance assessment?

    I am aware of several school systems that have begun the process of refining their curriculum and standards to align with the new state standards. I know that this activity must involve the entire staff if it is to impact instruction.

2. What have I heard about or observed that especially interests me?

    I have heard about a backward planning model and several technology-enabled solutions that might help achieve my goal.

3. What would I like to do differently?

    I am committed to having this be an involvement and not a compliance process.

4. What are my wants and needs for my professional life?

    I want to find a way to have staff members see the goals of the school plan as a challenge, become comfortable with continual change and improvement, and not feel threatened by new ideas. I have learned to accept the challenge of change in my professional and personal life and hope that I can find the tools and patience to facilitate that understanding among staff members.

REFINING THE BANNER QUESTION   ■

Occasionally the need arises to revise the banner question. School leaders may find themselves starting in one direction with their banner question, and then discovering another area of greater urgency or need. Or often the first stab at a banner question produces a question that is too broad, and the school leader realizes that he or she has a more specific need to address. A banner question is not set in stone. LPS participants should seek assistance from their LPS partners or the roundtable group to refine their banner question.

The sample banner questions in Figure 3.6 offer examples of the focusing process. After focusing the goals of the LPS, the next phase of the LPS process is developing a LPS plan and a process for participation and learning through collaboration with one's colleagues.

Figure 3.6

Sample Banner Questions

The following examples demonstrate the range of banner questions created by school leaders who have participated in the LPS. These questions emerged through reflective roundtable conversations among one group of school leaders. Each became a banner question and the focus for a school leader's portfolio.

- How can I serve as a change agent and still meet the needs of a varied constituency?

- How can I serve as a change agent and meet mandates and assessment demands?

- How can the emphasis on assessment stimulate improvement in curriculum and instruction?

- What constitutes professional growth?

- Will improving the quality of relationships within the school community contribute to our goal of helping all students succeed intellectually and personally?

- Does instructional technology improve student learning?

- How can technology enhance learning?

- How can we deal more effectively with the needs of our increasingly diverse school population?

- Is educational change possible without a common educational purpose?

- How can I support and encourage an integrated curriculum?

- How can we combine multiple methods of evaluation to support learning and comply with accountability demands?

- What is the purpose and function of education in the global workplace?

- How can I build community support, awareness, and involvement in these times of uncertainty regarding the future of education?

■   **SUMMARY OF LPS CONTENTS**

At the end of the second phase of the LPS process you will have completed the following:

From Phase One—Purpose and Function for Work

- Written definition of leadership standards, attributes, and expectations
- Agreement on Purpose
- Defining Your Theory of Action

From Phase Two—Focus for Learning

- Focused Leadership diagram
- Establishing Targeted Priority Goals
- Benchmarks and checkpoints
- Banner Question

4

The Process and Structures for Collaborations

ESTABLISHING PROFESSIONAL STRUCTURES FOR COLLABORATIONS ■

After establishing the LPS purpose and focus, the next phase of the LPS is process. In this phase school leaders identify the process for action planning and professional structures for collaborating with others and engaging in learning activities. In this phase, school leaders identify existing professional structures such as the following:

- Principal meetings
- Leadership team roundtables
- One-on-ones with the superintendent or supervisor
- Coaching or mentoring sessions

These structures can provide the professional learning environment necessary to support the leader in his or her learning and performance planning. (See Figure 4.2 in Appendix C and Figure 4.3 in Appendix D.) Tapping into existing structures as a venue for collaboration helps integrate the LPS with current practices. If these structures do not currently exist the leader can consider establishing collaborations to facilitate and support their learning and selection of professional learning activities—activities and professional structures that align with and inform their banner question and performance goals. Each step in the LPS process helps school leaders develop and enhance their abilities.

■ IDENTIFYING AN LPS PARTNER

One of the most powerful learning opportunities in the LPS process is establishment of a peer coaching relationship with a colleague who is also using the LPS process. LPS partners help each other with specific areas for professional growth by listening, asking questions, and offering assistance and encouragement through all phases of the process. Some LPS participants prefer partners; others prefer working in a team. Working with a partner and as part of a team is the most effective and efficient combination because it offers frequent, informal meetings with a single peer coach and the benefit of numerous viewpoints and ideas from the larger group. Often, a combination of frequent, as needed partner meetings several times during the term and meeting as a group helps everyone "check in."

■ BENEFITS OF PEER COLLABORATION

The key to transforming and growing with the work rather than just doing the job is to commit to trusting, sustained relationships with colleagues. Such relationships improve professional learning, encourage feedback, and promote progress in the school system. The challenge is building trusting relationships in which peers can rely on each other for support, information, and feedback. Successful relationships demand a time commitment, which allows for meetings where school leaders can talk about work challenges, successes, and failures. To ensure continued success, members must also commit to sustaining the relationship.

> The key to transforming and growing is to commit to trusting, sustained relationships with colleagues.

LPS partners help school leaders lay foundations for building trusting relationships within their school systems. The more informal relationship among partners allows for conversations that might begin, "How did the meeting go?" "Have you been able to get closer to an agreement with the teacher's union?" "How about lunch Thursday?" "We can work on our challenge of linking student learning to professional development."

Partner meetings should remain informal and occur as needed. Partners can use the meetings to reflect on daily decisions and other experiences related to their banner questions. They can also discuss similar needs and goals, their purpose for the LPS process, each leader's scope of leadership, and how they can support each other. Other activities collaborators might pursue are to

- discuss current, pressing issues and decision making regarding prioritizing goals;
- review current accountability demands and plans for improving student achievement;

- refine the banner question;
- consider which professional development activities to pursue;
- share learning plans and performance goals and make adaptations;
- make plans to observe the partner conduct meetings and workshops;
- ask for feedback or input regarding a past or upcoming decision;
- ask for suggestions regarding activities in their professional performance plan;
- share data for reporting results and evidence of learning from the LPS engagement;
- share current research findings and learning.

SCHEDULING ROUNDTABLE SESSIONS ■

For the leadership LPS process to have impact across all systems within a school or district, school leaders need to come together to reflect and collaborate. The roundtable provides LPS participants with an opportunity to work together several times during the term to share progress, pose questions, and refocus their learning.

The roundtable may be a part of an existing structure such as a work team, a district office leadership group, or a site-level leadership team. In some districts, a roundtable is composed of LPS partners who share similar purposes and banner questions. Ideal group size is six to eight participants.

It helps to set an agreed upon schedule for roundtable sessions at the beginning of the LPS process. Setting themes for the roundtable sessions based on the four LPS phases assists in pacing participants through the process and focusing the conversations during the sessions. Roundtable sessions usually last one to two hours. Leaders who once claimed they did not have the time or discipline to collaborate, reflect, and learn together find the roundtable discussions invaluable. Figure 4.1 offers a sample set of roundtable discussion topics.

Throughout the LPS process, it is vital to remember the importance of building trusting relationships. As Wheatley (1992) reminded us, if relationships work, the work goes well. It is the trusting relationships, the shared purpose, and the continual sharing and restructuring of information that guides school systems into this era of knowledge sharing. The LPS process gives school leaders practice and experience in all three areas.

Figure 4.1

Sample Roundtable Discussion Plan

Establishing themes for roundtable sessions sets the pace for the term and helps participants assess the final outcomes from the LPS process at the end of the term.

Define LPS purpose and district assessment parameters.

- Share Agreement on Purpose worksheets.
- Clarify agreement regarding assessment and collaboration.
- Agree on process for the LPS.

Formulate banner question and splinter questions.

- Discuss banner questions and help clarify interest, purpose, need, and so forth.
- Consider possible splinter questions.
- Consider possible themes emerging from banner question and splinter questions.

Collect data and evidence.

- Identify indicators for assessing progress toward and success with goals.
- Review and discuss data, artifacts, and evidence.
- Clarify questions, observations, and learning.

Design professional development plan.

- Discuss current activities and what they might contribute to the plan.
- Offer suggestions for additional professional development activities.
- Clarify connections among activities, LPS themes, and work goals.

Assess partner meetings.

- Review progress with partner meeting sessions.
- Consider additional collaborations such as peer coaching.
- Discuss collaborations that are working and those that are not to receive feedback and suggestions.

Evaluate the effectiveness of the LPS process.

- Reflect on the most effective parts of the LPS process.
- Invite suggestions to improve process in this setting.
- Establish focus for next roundtable.

Figure 4.2

Professional Structures for Collaboration Survey

STRUCTURE	PURPOSE/FACILITATOR	PARTICIPANTS	SCHEDULE

Figure 4.3

Sample Professional Structures for Collaboration Survey

Sample High School

STRUCTURE	PURPOSE/FACILITATOR	PARTICIPANTS	SCHEDULE
School Leadership Meeting	Coordinate and monitor results for six small schools. Make decisions to keep on course and make adaptations in policies and practices as indicated.	Principals Dir. C & I and PD Facilities Manager Student Services Superintendent Community Service	Mondays 4:00-6:00
School Site Council (SSC)	An advisory Board that can influence the decision-making process with the Board of Directors	2 Principals 2 Parents 2 Teachers	Site determines
Late Start Days	Professional Development and Common Planning Time	Faculty	Professional Development 1st Thursdays 3rd Common Planning 8:00-11:00
Staff Meetings/ Small Schools	Each small school designs their agenda based on priorities and needs	Principal and faculty	Tuesdays 3:15-4:00
Staff Meetings/ Depts.	Agendas and facilitation rotated by staff members who monitor facilities, communications, and other operational duties	Department members	Site determines
Accountability Team	Aligns funding and performance goals set by the Board and staff with NCLB	Accountability Team members	Monthly, 3rd Tuesdays, 10:00-11:30
Small School Autonomy Committee (SSAC)	Implements recommendations and facilitation of on-going dialogue concerning small school autonomy.	Policy authors Superintendent Reps. from each small school	4 times a year time Date TBD
Leadership Round Table	Round Table reviews goals and learnings, as well as alignments among activities, and makes recommendations for next steps.	LPS participants	Monthly on 2nd Tuesdays, 10:00-11:30.

SUMMARY OF LPS CONTENTS   ■

At the end of the third phase of the LPS process, the LPS contains the following materials:

From Phase One—Purpose and Function for Work

- Written definition of leadership standards, attributes, and expectations
- Agreement on Purpose
- Defining Your Theory of Action

From Phase Two—Focus for Learning

- Focused Leadership diagram
- Establishing Targeted Priority Goals
- Benchmarks and checkpoints
- Banner Question

From Phase Three—Process and Structures of Collaboration

- Identifying current professional structures and LPS partner
- Establishing leadership roundtable discussion plan

5

Outcomes for Action Planning and Reporting Results

TAKING ACTION ■

A school plan should address the following essential areas:

- Goals—a translation of the district goals into school goals and priorities
- Budget—funds available for prioritized efforts
- Timeline—time required to implement the plan and a schedule of checkpoints to monitor progress and maintain focus on priority efforts
- Needs assessment—Needs assessment-determining priority goals based on student data analysis and knowing the readiness level of the staff, both psychologically and cognitively using; the research-based Concerns-Based Adoption Model (CBAM) will provide clarity and direction for determining the willingness and abilities of staff for change; the model offers descriptors and strategies to determine readiness, demonstrated by the individual's level of concern regarding a change in practice and the level of use as demonstrated in their current capacity for new practices.

- Opportunities and resources—funding available for implementing and sustaining priority efforts
- Success indicators—collection of evidence and data that demonstrate the successful outcomes of action plans
- Professional learning—the needs of the school leader's work and their personal desires and needs for learning; school leaders must determine needs related to district/school targeted priorities and expertise that would enhance and inform their performance and seek to combine their professional and performance goals.

■ CREATING A PROFESSIONAL PERFORMANCE PLAN

The school leader's performance plan uses results of Defining Your Theory of Action, the focused leadership performance goals, school action planning with targeted priority goals, and the Banner Question worksheet to plan formal and informal professional development opportunities. In their performance plan, school leaders list professional development activities, evidence, outcomes, and reflections as well as applications of professional learning to their work.

At this time, school leaders list the professional development activities in which they are currently involved. They continue to add activities to the plan as they move through the LPS process and collaborate with others. School leaders might consider keeping a professional development activity log to record suggestions, contacts, and information sources for professional development activities and share results at roundtable sessions. A Professional Development Activities Log appears in Figure 5.1 and also in Appendix C. Examples of common professional development activities follow:

- Visit other schools to observe new practices in action (e.g., block scheduling in a high school or grade level team planning in an elementary school) and learn how these new ideas and practices were organized and successfully implemented.
- Attend seminars.
- Meet with others who have similar goals and professional interests.
- Observe teaching and group facilitation in progress and take notes for later reflection.
- Invite a colleague to observe a staff meeting or workshop the school leader conducts.
- Read articles in professional journals.
- Join a study group whose focus is related to the leader's goals.
- Research information related to the banner question.
- Join a professional organization for school leaders.

The next steps in this phase follow:

- Select a LPS partner who acts as peer coach and helps with specific areas for professional growth.

- Identify specific areas for learning, research, and expansion of knowledge related to the banner question.
- Establish success indicators for the goals set in phase two.
- Schedule roundtable discussions to reflect and collaborate on learning with other LPS participants.

Figure 5.1 is an example of a Professional Development Activities Log, and Figure 5.2 is an example of one school leader's activity log based on the following banner question: how can I enhance our district's capacity to build a standards-based curriculum and respond to accountability demands? This school leader has completed some of these activities and has listed target dates for those she plans to complete during the school year. (A copy of the completed log also appears in Appendix D.)

Identify Areas for Learning

LPS partners can help each other Identify Areas of Learning, research, and expansion of knowledge. Partners may ask each other questions such as the following:

- What do you want to know more about?
- What do you want to be able to do?
- What will help you reach your goals for the term?
- What type of learning environment will help you improve your skills?

For example, an assistant superintendent creates the following banner question: What is the balance between participating in professional development activities and meeting accountability demands for performance among educators? She intends to use the LPS as part of her evaluation process. As she has responsibilities in the area of personnel, one of her goals is establishing an effective professional development model in the district and negotiating with the teacher's union to include professional development and alternative teacher assessments in the teachers' new contract. One of the items for discussion is teachers using the LPS process as a form of alternative assessment that also promotes professional growth. The school leader and her LPS partner might discuss what information she needs to accomplish her goal. With whom might she visit or talk to gain new understanding or see models to consider?

Collect Evidence

Artifacts and evidence are success indicators in the LPS process. Artifacts represent an incident or lesson that was significant to the learning process. Evidence consists of data and concrete illustrations that validate and confirm the learning and findings that take place through the LPS process.

As school leaders collect artifacts and evidence, they might record them in a registry to establish an ongoing profile of their learning journey.

Figure 5.1

Professional Development Activities Log

Date _____   Activity _____

_____

_____

_____

_____

_____

_____

_____

_____

_____

_____

_____

_____

_____

_____

_____

_____

_____

_____

Figure 5.2

Sample Professional Development Activities Log

Date _____   Activity _____

Done:

10/06   *I read* Understanding by Design *by Wiggins and McTighe (1998).*

10/06   *I observed my LPS partner to watch interaction with staff.*

11/06   *I visited a school where staff members use a standards-based curriculum.*

2/07   *I read* Stewardship: Choosing Service over Self-Interest *by Block (1993).*

To do:

2/07   *Build plan for establishing an action research project for performance assessments.*

3/07   *Attend Conference on Intelligent Behavior.*

4/07   *Attend Association for Supervision and Curriculum Development (ASCD) national conference.*

4/07   *Enroll in Leadership in the Future class at the university.*

5/07   *Participate in community planning project.*

5/07   *Attend State Administrator Association conference.*

5/07   *Read* Mapping the Big Picture: Integrating Curriculum and Assessment K–12 *by Jacobs (1997).*

5/07   *Read* Performance Assessment and Standards-based Curricula *by Glatthorn, Bragaw, Dawkins, and Parker (1998).*

Many LPS users have found tools such as the Evidence Registry (Figure 5.3) and the Professional Development Activities Log (Figure 5.1) very helpful during their first experience with the LPS process. (See the template of the registry in Figure 5.3 and in Appendix C.) In subsequent years, they organize and move through the process by focusing mainly on a banner question and the reflective collaborations. School leaders should use the tools and worksheets the book offers if they help focus and facilitate movement through the process but put the tools aside if they become a chore or a distraction to learning. Those school leaders who at some point decide to construct an employment LPS and use the LPS process as part of their professional assessment will find that the tools provide structure and records for the assessment process. Figure 5.3 is an example of an Evidence Registry, and Figure 5.4 is one school leader's completed Evidence Registry. (Copies of these also appear in Appendix D.)

Remember, artifacts and evidence are not the same. The following story about an artifact collected by a first-year administrator highlights the difference.

Administrator A was one of three administrators in a high school. All thirty-five administrators in the district were participating in the LPS process. They met in their roundtable sessions every two weeks. This administrator's primary area of responsibility and her goals focused on maintenance and improvement of physical buildings and grounds and improving school climate and morale. Her banner question was "How can I improve the physical environment at our high school?" Her plan was to involve students, teachers, other staff members, and ultimately, community members. At the second roundtable session, she shared her frustrations about staff members' unwillingness to participate on a committee or even contribute ideas to improve the campus. Her colleagues asked her coaching questions such as who in your immediate scope of reporting might help you and what would be a good place to begin improvements?

> Artifacts and evidence are success indicators in the LPS process.

Administrator A was sure that the school's groundskeeper was the answer to both these questions. Her peers suggested she ask the groundskeeper what he needed to begin the improvement process and where he recommended that the two of them begin. Together, they decided to begin by cleaning up the bushes and trees around the edge of the campus. The groundskeeper needed a chain saw to remove low branches from the trees. One bright morning, the chain saw buzzed off the lower limbs of the trees, and by noon, the administrator had an office full of students complaining that the space was destroyed. It turns out that the branches were great protection for unauthorized smoking during class breaks. The surprising experience that Administrator A had after the groundskeeper trimmed the trees led to a positive aftermath. The students wanted to be involved from that point on. By the end of the term, community members joined forces with the art teacher and students in rendering a mural on the outside gymnasium wall. The campus was transformed. The artifact this administrator brought to reflect on at the closing roundtable was the chain saw.

Figure 5.3

Evidence Registry

Briefly list any artifact or evidence that causes reflection and prompts collaboration related to your banner question.

_____

_____

_____

_____

_____

_____

_____

_____

_____

_____

_____

_____

_____

_____

_____

_____

_____

Figure 5.4

Sample Evidence Registry

This school leader collected data in response to the banner question "How can I enhance our district's capacity to build a standards-based curriculum and respond to accountability demands?"

Briefly list any artifact or evidence that causes reflection and prompts collaboration related to your banner question.

Student data from action research

Initial proposal from teacher's union for negotiations

Reflections from reading Stewardship

Model of a scale representing the delicacy of balance in work and in life

Copy of district standards for administrators

Standards for professional development from National Staff Development Council

Samples of curriculum backward planning using Understanding by Design

Design for assessing current state of grade-level curriculum and aligning with standards

Coaching models for building grade-level teams

■ OUTCOMES—REPORTING RESULTS

Following the collection of data and the compilation of evidence, it is time to reflect on the LPS experience. Depending on the goals and banner questions, summaries and reflections could include data results, observations regarding these results, as well as a direction for the next steps in the LPS process. This is the time to use the LPS information as the vehicle for evolving the LPS and for extending professional development, refining goals, and effecting change.

Figure 5.5 is a template with suggested reflections and questions to respond to as you bring closure to your LPS process, and Figure 5.6 is one school leader's completed Outcomes of the LPS Process. (See Appendix.) Note the templates or forms usually appear in a different Appendix as the completed forms. Appendix C has templates and Appendix D has completed forms. This edition has a CD and features a Resource Matrix.

Figure 5.5

Outcomes of the LPS Process

Write your reflections on the LPS process.

What articulation, sharing, demonstrating, and exhibiting have you done regarding your LPS process and evidence of accomplishments?

What new questions have emerged from your engagement in the process?

How have your beliefs and assumptions been challenged or changed?

What are the emerging needs, requirements, and challenges for your next LPS?

Figure 5.6

Sample Outcomes of the LPS Process

Write your reflections on the LPS process.

Participating in the LPS process has provided an opportunity to learn, reflect, and make important connections with other educational leaders both in and out of our system. I began this year with an extreme feeling of pressure regarding the charge of building a standards-based curriculum and linking it to performance assessment. I was determined to find a way to make this more than a task. I really wanted to see a shift in instruction and for the teachers to own and share this challenge. Participation in the roundtable gave me the energy and courage to try and do this the RIGHT way. I presented to the school board the option for building a standards-based curriculum. We could produce a document that contains a neatly organized curriculum aligned to the standards, or we could engage the teachers in the process of designing a standards-based curriculum that assists us in striving to improve and drastically modify what and how we teach and assess. The second option has the potential to build teacher capacity for teaching to the standards. Producing a curriculum document does not assure a change in instruction. There is a greater likelihood that instruction will shift if teachers are engaged in the design process.

With the sponsorship in the school system and the support of the board, we took the teacher-as-professional route. It is paying off. It has been a leadership challenge to focus on building capacity and commitment and letting go of the control and compliance. I have learned a great deal about myself and my need for feedback from others. The professional network we have established will continue to be an asset in my work. Collecting artifacts and evidence to share also helped me in pacing and focusing my work. Aiming for goals was important, but doing the work, with permission to adapt and facilitate the process with staff members, was where the bulk of my energy was spent. As a result of working through the portfolio process, I have come to realize the impact of isolation on my work as well as the verve that entered my work as I opened myself and my professional workspace to others.

What articulation, sharing, demonstrating, and exhibiting have you done regarding your LPS process and evidence of accomplishments?

I have shared my LPS with members of my roundtable and with my LPS partner. I also belong to a local administrator association where I have shared the model I developed for building a standards-based curriculum. These demonstrations have opened the door for new information and resources regarding the performance assessments, our next big challenge in the school system!

What new questions have emerged from your engagement in the process?

As a result of participation in the LPS process, I am seeking new ways to define and describe professional development. I am asking questions about the evaluation of educators—teachers and administrators. What is the purpose and function of the evaluation process, and is it accomplishing that purpose in its current form?

How have your beliefs and assumptions been challenged or changed?

The greatest challenge I have faced this year is finding the balance in my work and my life. I am continually perplexed about how we so often compromise or set aside our belief and our truth in the name of getting it done. That compliant mindset will not get us where we need to go with students. This belief is a constant with me, and the change might be that together we could accomplish a great deal.

What are the emerging needs, requirements, and challenges for your next LPS?

My performance goal for next year will be part two of what I started this year. I will move on to extended implementation and connecting performance assessment and multiple sources of student data to the new, standards-based curriculum.

SUMMARY OF LPS CONTENTS ■

At the end of the last two phases of the process, the LPS contains the following materials:

From Phase One—Purpose and Function for Work

- Written definition of leadership standards, attributes, and expectations
- Agreement on Purpose
- Defining Your Theory of Action

From Phase Two—Focus for Learning

- Focused Leadership diagram
- Establishing Targeted Priority Goals
- Benchmarks and checkpoints
- Banner Questions, key standards, and priority goals

From Phase Three—Process and Structures for Collaboration

- Identifying current professional structures and LPS partner
- Establishing leadership roundtable discussion plan
- Essentials for school/district action planning
- Establish a professional performance plan
- Maintaining a Professional Development Activities Log
- Collecting data and evidence

From Phase Four—Outcomes for Action Planning and Reporting Results

- Action planning
- Prepare summary and conclusions and share the following:
  (a) report results,
  (b) lessons learned,
  (c) observations regarding results and collaboration, and
  (d) next steps.

Figure 5.7

Primary Benefits and Lessons of the LPS

Benefits

Builds teams and collaborations

Facilitates and focuses learning

Invites feedback about effectiveness

Identifies contributions to school community

Connects learning with work

Lessons learned

Commitment is essential.

Scheduled time for collaboration is necessary.

Connections with work and other portfolio participants are powerful!

6

Technology and the LPS Process

EMPLOYING ELECTRONIC SUPPORT ▪

Technology supports each phase of the LPS (see Figure 6.1). School leaders can track their progress and capture their reflections electronically. They may use various technologies to collect and record information. Partners and teams may use connected technologies to communicate.

Technology and Purpose for Work

As school leaders meet to define their purpose and examine leadership attributes and standards, a recorder may note key ideas on a laptop computer and print it for distribution to group members. These notes will assist participants as they record their agreements on purpose and define their philosophy. They will continue to use these technology tools to enhance and streamline the process as they move on to the second phase of the process.

Technology and Focus for Learning

In developing a banner question, participants examine and reflect on district goals, school plans, and professional and personal learning goals and needs. They may use documents from their district or other information from Internet searches, storing documents, and results of searches on disks or a Zip drive.

As a group, they may use computer software to create visual organizers that assist in planning.

Formulating a banner question takes time, reflection, and collaborative conversations. While leaders may have many of these conversations in person, the group can also communicate by means of a conference phone call, videoconferences, or by participating in Internet blog discussions. Setting up a central site where electronic communication can occur will help ease time constraints for school leaders.

Technology and Process for Collaboration

During this phase, participants plan and collect artifacts and evidence regarding their learning and discuss their progress with an LPS partner. One partner might record suggestions, contacts, and information sources on a database; another partner might use Palm Pilot technology to record information. Both partners might use scanners and digital or video cameras to collect artifacts and record them in a computer registry or on a compact disc. When partners are unable to meet, they might send the artifact pictures and documents as e-mail attachments. Participants can use listservs to share information in remote roundtable discussions. (A listserv posts messages to each of the listserv subscribers through e-mail.)

Technology and Outcomes for Improvement

The outcomes phase of the LPS process allows leaders to synthesize their learning. It is a time of review and continuing reflection. If leaders have stored LPS evidence on disk, they can share it by using a data projector, electronic whiteboard, or even a Web site. This is a time to call upon technology to demonstrate, illustrate, and exhibit learning, as well as to identify next steps.

Figure 6.1

Technology Resource Guide for the Portfolio Process

LPS PHASE	KEY ACTIVITIES	TECHNOLOGY SUPPORT
Phase One: Purpose for Work	Define philosophy. Define leadership attributes. Define standards. Establish portfolio purpose.	Use computer word processing, e-mail, and Internet searches of district documents to clarify, combine, and formulate goals and essential questions.
Phase Two: Focus for Learning	Set goals. Develop a banner question.	Use computer word processing, e-mail, and the Internet to formulate, research, and clarify.
Phase Three: Process and Structures for Collaboration	Identify appropriate collaborative groups. Hold roundtable discussions.	Use a scanner, modem, digital camera, palm organizer, e-mail, conference calls, video cameras, and DVDs to share reflections, research, and information.
Phase Four: Outcomes for Action Planning and Reporting Results	Gather data and evidence Track benchmarks and checkpoints Assess and articulate learning. Decide next steps.	Use computers and software to track action plan progress and to document movement toward goals. Use computer presentation software and hardware or electronic whiteboards to illustrate and demonstrate learning and next steps.

Appendices

Contents

The following appendices contain materials on the leadership performance system (LPS) that are designed for reproduction for the reader's convenience.

LPS Resource Matrix

A Guide to Resources and Templates

RESOURCES	PURPOSE	FOCUS	PROCESS	OUTCOMES
LPS Portfolio Journal (See CD)	√	√	√	√
Leadership Performance System Model pp. xxiv, 70	√	√	√	√
ISLLC Standards and LPS Alignment pp. 3, 19	√	√	√	√
Technology Resource Guide p. 65	√	√	√	√
LPS Phases Process p. 69	√	√	√	√
Steps in the LPS Process p. 71	√	√	√	√
ISLLC Standards Resources p. 93	√	√	√	
TEMPLATES				
Steps in the LPS Process p. 71	√	√	√	√
Agreement on Purpose p. 74	√	√		
Defining Your Theory of Action p. 75	√	√		
Focused Leadership p. 76	√			
Establishing Targeted Priority Goals p. 77	√	√		
Banner Question Template p. 78		√		
Professional Structures for Collaboration Survey p. 79	√	√	√	
Professional Development Activities Log p. 80			√	
Evidence Registry p. 81			√	√
Outcomes of the LPS Process p. 82				√

√ Indicates alignment with portfolio phases; a valuable tool for users

Figure 1.3   LPS Process

Phases of the LPS

Purpose and Function

Theory of Action • Leadership Attributes and Standards

Focus for Learning

Goals • Banner Question

Process and Structures for Collaboration

Professional Learning Community • Feedback and Collaborations

Planning • Engagement • Collecting Evidence

Outcomes for Action Planning and Reporting Results

Action Plan • Assess Results • Reflect on Learnings • Set New Goals

Figure 0.1   Leadership Performance System

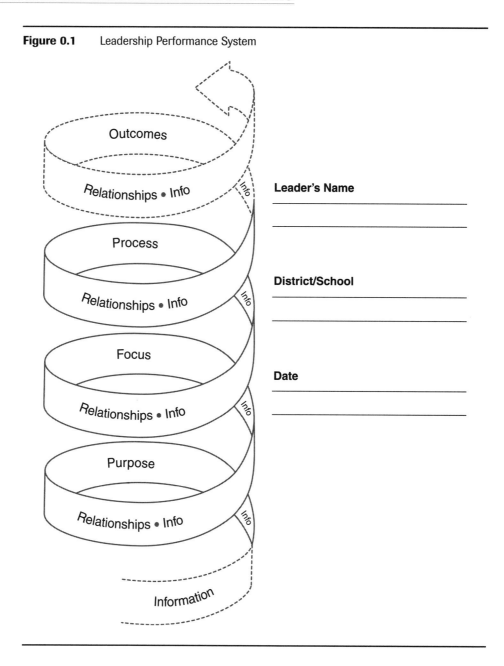

Figure 2.1

Steps in the LPS Process

The first three steps of the LPS process mark the school leader's introduction to the process and set the stage for the remainder of the process. Steps four through seven define ongoing activities, which take place throughout the LPS process.

Introduction to the LPS Process

Step 1: Participate in the initial purpose-setting session (phase one).

Step 2: Focus LPS by identifying goals and establishing banner question (phase two).

Step 3: Identify professional structures for collaborations and an LPS partner and a collaboration network, and begin process of collaboration and activities (phase three).

Ongoing Activities Within the LPS Process

Step 4: Set school/district and school administrator's professional development goals, establish learning plans, and collect artifacts and evidence (phases two and three).

Step 5: Design the Action Plan (phase four).

Step 6: Engage in roundtable sessions (phases one, two, three, and four).

Step 7: Evaluate outcomes and determine effectiveness of the process; make adaptations as indicated (phase four).

Templates of LPS Tools

Templates appear in the following order:

- Agreement on Purpose (Figure 2.4)
- Defining Your Theory of Action (Figure 2.6)
- Focused Leadership (Figure 3.1)
- Establishing Targeted Priority Goals (Figure 3.2)
- Banner Question (Figure 3.4)
- Professional Structures for Collaboration Survey (Figure 4.2)
- Professional Development Activities Log (Figure 5.1)
- Evidence Registry (Figure 5.3)
- Outcomes of the LPS Process (Figure 5.5)

Figure 2.4

Agreement on Purpose

From my point of view, the primary purpose of the LPS is as follows:

Collaboration and learning can enhance my work in the following ways:

I will consider my time and efforts with the LPS worthwhile if the following events occur:

Figure 2.6

Defining Your Theory of Action

Take this opportunity to reflect on your Theory of Action, and then share your perspectives with a partner or member of your roundtable.

What beliefs do you hold about the purpose and function of leadership?

Describe your perspective of a most effective management system or routine.

What beliefs do you hold about how people learn?

What are your top three priorities in your work?

Figure 3.1

Focused Leadership

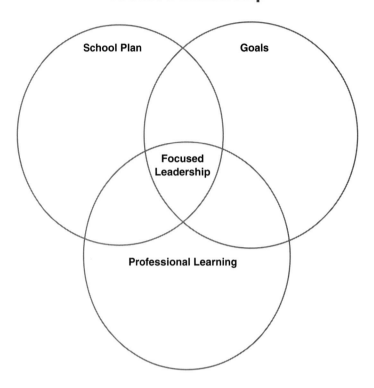

Figure 3.2

Establishing Targeted Priority Goals

The focus and priority goals for my professional work this year are as follows:

I currently have the following expertise and commitment to achieving these goals:

Specific strategies, skills, and expertise I would like to expand to be successful with implementing these instructional priorities are as follows:

Essential benchmarks for achievement toward my goals include the following:

Figure 3.4   Banner Question

Banner Question

Write your banner question here; remember that you can refine the question later.

Splinter Questions

What additional questions do you need to answer before you can answer your banner question?

1.   What do I already know about [banner question topic]?

2.   What have I heard about or observed that especially interests me?

3.   What would I like to do differently?

4.   What are my wants and needs for my professional life?

Figure 4.2

Professional Structures for Collaboration Survey

STRUCTURE	PURPOSE/FACILITATOR	PARTICIPANTS	SCHEDULE

Figure 5.1

Professional Development Activities Log

Date _____   Activity _____

_____

_____

_____

_____

_____

_____

_____

_____

_____

_____

_____

_____

_____

_____

_____

_____

_____

_____

_____

_____

_____

Figure 5.3

Evidence Registry

Briefly list any artifact or evidence that causes reflection and prompts collaboration related to your banner question.

_____

_____

_____

_____

_____

_____

_____

_____

_____

_____

_____

_____

_____

_____

_____

_____

_____

_____

Figure 5.5

Outcomes of the LPS Process

Write your reflections on the LPS process.

What articulation, sharing, demonstrating, and exhibiting have you done regarding your LPS process and evidence of accomplishments?

What new questions have emerged from your engagement in the process?

How have your beliefs and assumptions been challenged or changed?

What are the emerging needs, requirements, and challenges for your next LPS?

Sample Completed LPS Tools

Completed tools that serve as examples appear in the following order:

- Sample Agreement on Purpose (Figure 2.5)
- Sample Defining Your Theory of Action (Figure 2.7)
- Sample Establishing Targeted Priority Goals (Figure 3.3)
- Sample Banner Question (Figure 3.5)
- Sample Professional Structures for Collaboration (Figure 4.3)
- Sample Professional Development Activities Log (Figure 5.2)
- Sample Evidence Registry (Figure 5.4)
- Sample Outcomes of the LPS Process (Figure 5.6)

Figure 2.5

Sample Agreement on Purpose

From my point of view, the primary purpose of the LPS is as follows:

The purpose is to provide a structure and process for me and my colleagues to talk about our work. I would welcome an opportunity to have constructive feedback and, most of all, suggestions for working more effectively and efficiently. Another purpose that would serve my work would be to create an environment where we have less competition and more collaboration. The LPS can also serve as a documentation of my work and learning.

Collaboration and learning can enhance my work in the following ways:

I would like to know more about the work of others in our school system. I seem to be informed many times after the fact. Such collaboration can offer feedback and possibly more timely flow of information. I would benefit from sharing in efforts and past experiences of others in the school system. The challenge for us is to establish an environment for collaboration—one we have not always had in the past.

I will consider my time and efforts with the LPS worthwhile if the following events occur:

1. *We integrate the process into our current leadership meetings and assessment process.*

2. *We produce documents worthy of sharing when applying for future employment.*

3. *We build a collaboration network among leaders in our system.*

Figure 2.7

Sample Defining Your Theory of Action

Take this opportunity to reflect on your Theory of Action, and then share your perspectives with a partner or member of your roundtable.

What beliefs do you hold about the purpose and function of leadership?

The purpose of leadership is to create an environment for collaboration, commitment, and learning among the professionals and other staff members in the school system. Leaders do not have all the answers; they must develop, nurture, and draw on the expertise and wisdom of all members in the system.

Describe your perspective of a most effective management system or routine.

This is not my greatest area of strength. I have found setting goals annually is very important. When I have been disciplined enough to set goals for my work, I have been able to establish work plans to correspond with checkpoints, and the technique does seem to work. The challenge to this system is not overlooking the first step—focus and plan. Then the rest of the tactical aspects of the job seem to follow along.

What beliefs do you hold about how people learn?

I believe we learn in a very natural way, using experimentation and new information as well as prior experiences to try new things. It is through those interactions that we construct new understandings and expand our repertoire of knowledge. The information we take in to solve problems and meet new challenges adds to our knowledge and repertoire of understanding. Thus, it is a continuous process.

What are your top three priorities in your work?

My priorities are to build commitment and capacity among staff members, to offer a learner-centered instructional program, and to listen to community and other professional input regarding research, innovations, and global needs to prepare students for the future. As educators, we must first do no harm.

Figure 3.3

Sample Establishing Targeted Priority Goals

The focus and priority goals for my professional work this year are as follows:

- *Implement standards-based instruction in mathematics*
- *Use data to determine the appropriate instructional level for students*
- *Plan differentiated instruction about identified student needs*
- *Establish intervention strategies and study groups for students who are having a difficult time meeting the grade-level standards.*

I currently have the following expertise and commitment to achieving these goals:

As a teacher, I have designed differentiation strategies, in mathematics for students in my class. I will support my colleagues in analyzing their student data to determine the student grouping and instructional strategies to support accelerated achievement in mathematics.

Specific strategies, skills, and expertise I would like to expand to be successful with implementing these instructional priorities are as follows:

I would like to have new formative assessments that we could use as a grade level team to monitor progress and inform our instructional planning in mathematics. I would also like to work with my grade level and mathematics team in determining their professional development needs to build an action plan around these priority goals targeted at student achievement.

Essential benchmarks for achievement toward my goals include the following:

I will with my team and look at student data to reach agreement in realistic benchmarks and scheduled checkpoints to update progress with the design, implementation, and progress with the goals.

Figure 3.5   Completed Banner Question

Banner Question

Write your banner question here; remember that you can refine the question later.

How can I use the mandate to design and implement standards-based curriculum with performance assessments as an opportunity to enhance and expand student learning?

Splinter Questions

What additional questions do you need to answer before you can answer your banner question?

- *What are successful models for performance assessments?*

- *What additional skills and training will staff members need to design a standards-based curriculum?*

- *What information and experience will they need to understand and use performance assessments?*

- *How will we modify our report card to reflect the new assessments and curriculum?*

- *To what degree will we need to modify our current instructional model?*

- *What new instruction materials will we need to make the curriculum shift?*

1. What do I already know about a standards-based curriculum and performance assessment?

    I am aware of several school systems that have begun the process of refining their curriculum and standards to align with the new state standards. I know that this activity must involve the entire staff if it is to impact instruction.

2. What have I heard about or observed that especially interests me?

    I have heard about a backward planning model and several technology-enabled solutions that might help achieve my goal.

3. What would I like to do differently?

    I am committed to having this be an involvement and not a compliance process.

4. What are my wants and needs for my professional life?

    I want to find a way to have staff members see the goals of the school plan as a challenge, become comfortable with continual change and improvement, and not feel threatened by new ideas. I have learned to accept the challenge of change in my professional and personal life and hope that I can find the tools and patience to facilitate that understanding among staff members.

Figure 4.3

Sample Professional Structures for Collaboration Survey

Sample High School

STRUCTURE	PURPOSE/FACILITATOR	PARTICIPANTS	SCHEDULE
School Leadership Meeting	Coordinate and monitor results for six small schools. Make decisions to keep on course and make adaptations in policies and practices as indicated.	Principals Dir. C & I and PD Facilities Manager Student Services Superintendent Community Service	Mondays 4:00-6:00
School Site Council (SSC)	An advisory Board that can influence the decision-making process with the Board of Directors	2 Principals 2 Parents 2 Teachers	Site determines
Late Start Days	Professional Development and Common Planning Time	Faculty	Professional Development 1st Thursdays 3rd Common Planning 8:00-11:00
Staff Meetings/ Small Schools	Each small school designs their agenda based on priorities and needs	Principal and faculty	Tuesdays 3:15-4:00
Staff Meetings/ Depts.	Agendas and facilitation rotated by staff members who monitor facilities, communications, and other operational duties	Department members	Site determines
Accountability Team	Aligns funding and performance goals set by the Board and staff with NCLB	Accountability Team members	Monthly, 3rd Tuesdays, 10:00-11:30
Small School Autonomy Committee (SSAC)	Implements recommendations and facilitation of on-going dialogue concerning small school autonomy.	Policy authors Superintendent Reps. from each small school	4 times a year time Date TBD
Leadership Round Table	Round Table reviews goals and learnings, as well as alignments among activities, and makes recommendations for next steps.	LPS participants	Monthly on 2nd Tuesdays, 10:00-11:30.

Figure 5.2

Sample Professional Development Activities Log

Date _____ Activity _____

Done:

10/06   *I read* Understanding by Design *by Wiggins and McTighe (1998).*

10/06   *I observed my LPS partner to watch interaction with staff.*

11/06   *I visited a school where staff members use a standards-based curriculum.*

2/07   *I read* Stewardship: Choosing Service over Self-Interest *by Block (1993).*

To do:

2/07   *Build plan for establishing an action research project for performance assessments.*

3/07   *Attend Conference on Intelligent Behavior.*

4/07   *Attend Association for Supervision and Curriculum Development (ASCD) national conference.*

4/07   *Enroll in Leadership in the Future class at the university.*

5/07   *Participate in community planning project.*

5/07   *Attend State Administrator Association conference.*

5/07   *Read* Mapping the Big Picture: Integrating Curriculum and Assessment K–12 by Jacobs (1997).

5/07   *Read* Performance Assessment and Standards-based Curricula *by Glatthorn, Bragaw, Dawkins, and Parker (1998).*

Figure 5.4

Sample Evidence Registry

This school leader collected data in response to the banner question "How can I enhance our district's capacity to build a standards-based curriculum and respond to accountability demands?"

Briefly list any artifact or evidence that causes reflection and prompts collaboration related to your banner question.

Student data from action research

Initial proposal from teacher's union for negotiations

Reflections from reading Stewardship

Model of a scale representing the delicacy of balance in work and in life

Copy of district standards for administrators

Standards for professional development from National Staff Development Council

Samples of curriculum backward planning using Understanding by Design

Design for assessing current state of grade-level curriculum and aligning with standards

Coaching models for building grade-level teams

Figure 5.6

Sample Outcomes of the LPS Process

Write your reflections on the LPS process.

Participating in the LPS process has provided an opportunity to learn, reflect, and make important connections with other educational leaders both in and out of our system. I began this year with an extreme feeling of pressure regarding the charge of building a standards-based curriculum and linking it to performance assessment. I was determined to find a way to make this more than a task. I really wanted to see a shift in instruction and for the teachers to own and share this challenge. Participation in the roundtable gave me the energy and courage to try and do this the RIGHT way. I presented to the school board the option for building a standards-based curriculum. We could produce a document that contains a neatly organized curriculum aligned to the standards, or we could engage the teachers in the process of designing a standards-based curriculum that assists us in striving to improve and drastically modify what and how we teach and assess. The second option has the potential to build teacher capacity for teaching to the standards. Producing a curriculum document does not assure a change in instruction. There is a greater likelihood that instruction will shift if teachers are engaged in the design process.

With the sponsorship in the school system and the support of the board, we took the teacher-as-professional route. It is paying off. It has been a leadership challenge to focus on building capacity and commitment and letting go of the control and compliance. I have learned a great deal about myself and my need for feedback from others. The professional network we have established will continue to be an asset in my work. Collecting artifacts and evidence to share also helped me in pacing and focusing my work. Aiming for goals was important, but doing the work, with permission to adapt and facilitate the process with staff members, was where the bulk of my energy was spent. As a result of working through the portfolio process, I have come to realize the impact of isolation on my work as well as the verve that entered my work as I opened myself and my professional workspace to others.

What articulation, sharing, demonstrating, and exhibiting have you done regarding your LPS process and evidence of accomplishments?

I have shared my LPS with members of my roundtable and with my LPS partner. I also belong to a local administrator association where I have shared the model I developed for building a standards-based curriculum. These demonstrations have opened the door for new information and resources regarding the performance assessments, our next big challenge in the school system!

What new questions have emerged from your engagement in the process?

As a result of participation in the LPS process, I am seeking new ways to define and describe professional development. I am asking questions about the evaluation of educators—teachers and administrators. What is the purpose and function of the evaluation process, and is it accomplishing that purpose in its current form?

How have your beliefs and assumptions been challenged or changed?

The greatest challenge I have faced this year is finding the balance in my work and my life. I am continually perplexed about how we so often compromise or set aside our belief and our truth in the name of getting it done. That compliant mindset will not get us where we need to go with students. This belief is a constant with me, and the change might be that together we could accomplish a great deal.

What are the emerging needs, requirements, and challenges for your next LPS?

My performance goal for next year will be part two of what I started this year. I will move on to extended implementation and connecting performance assessment and multiple sources of student data to the new, standards-based curriculum.

Interstate School Leaders Licensure Consortium (ISLLC) Standards for School Leaders

For background on the Interstate School Leaders Licensure Consortium (ISLLC) standards and for the process through which they arrived at these standards, visit the Council of Chief State School Officers Web site at http://www.ccsso.org/content/pdfs/isllcstd.pdf.

Standard 1

A school administrator is an educational leader who promotes the success of all students by facilitating the development, articulation, implementation, and stewardship of a vision of learning that is shared and supported by the school community.

The administration has knowledge and understanding of

- learning goals in a pluralistic society;
- the principles of developing and implementing strategic plans;
- systems theory;
- information sources, data collection, and data analysis strategies;
- effective communication;
- effective consensus-building and negotiation skills.

The administrator believes in, values, and is committed to

- the educability of all;
- a school vision of high standards of learning;
- continuous school improvement;
- the inclusion of all members of the school community;
- ensuring that students have the knowledge, skills, and values needed to become successful adults;
- a willingness to continuously examine one's own assumptions, beliefs, and practices;
- doing the work required for high levels of personal and organizational performance.

The administrator facilitates processes, and engages in activities ensuring that

- the vision and mission of the school are effectively communicated to staff, parents, students, and community members;
- the vision and mission are communicated through the use of symbols, ceremonies, stories, and similar activities;
- the core beliefs of the school vision are modeled for all stakeholders;
- the vision is developed with and among stakeholders;
- the contributions of school community members to the realization of the vision are recognized and celebrated;
- progress toward the vision and mission is communicated to all stakeholders;

- the school community is involved in school improvement efforts;
- the vision shapes the educational programs, plans, and activities;
- the vision shapes the educational programs, plans, and actions;
- an implementation plan is developed in which objectives and strategies to achieve the vision and goals are clearly articulated;
- assessment data related to student learning are used to develop the school vision and goals;
- relevant demographic data pertaining to students and their families are used in developing the school mission and goals;
- barriers to achieving the vision are identified, clarified, and addressed;
- needed resources are sought and obtained to support the implementation of the school mission and goals;
- existing resources are used in support of the school vision and goals;
- the vision, mission, and implementation plans are regularly monitored, evaluated, and revised.

Standard 2

A school administrator is an educational leader who promotes the success of all students by advocating, nurturing, and sustaining a school culture and instructional program conducive to student learning and staff professional growth.

The administrator has knowledge and understanding of

- student growth and development;
- applied learning theories;
- applied motivational theories;
- curriculum design, implementation, evaluation, and refinement;
- principles of effective instruction;
- measurement, evaluation, and assessment strategies;
- diversity and its meaning for educational programs;
- adult learning and professional development models;
- the change process for systems, organizations, and individuals;
- the role of technology in promoting student learning and professional growth;
- school cultures.

The administrator believes in, values, and is committed to

- student learning as the fundamental purpose of schooling;
- the proposition that all student can learn;
- the variety of ways in which students can learn;
- lifelong learning for self and others;
- professional development as an integral part of school improvement;
- the benefits that diversity brings to the school community;
- a safe and supportive learning environment;
- preparing students to be contributing members of society.

The administrator facilitates processes and engages in activities ensuring that

- all individuals are treated with fairness, dignity, and respect;
- professional development promotes a focus on student learning consistent with the school vision and goals;
- students and staff feel valued and important;
- the responsibilities and contributions of each individual are acknowledged;
- barriers to student learning are identified, clarified, and addressed;
- diversity is considered in developing learning experiences;
- lifelong learning is encouraged and modeled;
- there is a culture of high expectations for self, student, and staff performance;
- technologies are used in teaching and learning;
- student and staff accomplishments are recognized and celebrated;
- multiple opportunities to learn are available to all students;
- the school is organized and aligned for success;
- curricular, cocurricular, and extracurricular programs are designed, implemented, evaluated, and refined;
- curriculum decisions are based on research, expertise of teachers, and the recommendations of learned societies;
- the school culture and climate are assessed on a regular basis;
- a variety of sources of information is used to make decisions;
- student learning is assessed using a variety of techniques;
- multiple sources of information regarding performance are used by staff and students;
- a variety of supervisory and evaluation models is employed;
- pupil personnel programs are developed to meet the needs of students and their families.

Standard 3

A school administrator is an educational leader who promotes the success of all students by ensuring management of the organization, operations, and resources for a safe, efficient, and effective learning environment.

The administrator has knowledge and understanding of

- theories and models of organizations and the principles of organizational development;
- operational procedures at the school and district level;
- principles and issues relating to school safety and security;
- human resources managements and development;
- principles and issues relating to fiscal operations of school management;
- principles and issues relating to school facilities and use of space;
- legal issues impacting school operations;
- current technologies that support management functions.

The administrator believes in, values, and is committed to

- making management decisions to enhance learning and teaching;
- taking risks to improve schools;
- trusting people and their judgments;
- accepting responsibility;
- high-quality standards, expectations, and performances;
- involving stakeholders in management processes;
- a safe environment.

The administrator facilitates processes and engages in activities ensuring that

- knowledge of learning, teaching, and student development is used to inform management decisions;
- operational procedures are designed and managed to maximize opportunities for successful learning;
- emerging trends are recognized, studied, and applied as appropriate;
- operational plans and procedures to achieve the vision and goals of the school are in place;
- collective bargaining and other contractual agreements related to the school are effectively managed;
- the school plant, equipment, and support systems operate safely, efficiently, and effectively;
- time is managed to maximize attainment of organizational goals;
- potential problems and opportunities are identified;
- problems are confronted and resolved in a timely manner;
- financial, human, and material resources are aligned to the goals of schools;
- the school acts entrepreneurially to support continuous improvement;
- organizational systems are regularly monitored and modified as needed;
- stakeholders are involved in decisions affecting schools;
- responsibility is shared to maximize ownership and accountability;
- effective problem-framing and problem-solving skills are used;
- effective conflict resolutions skills are used;
- effective group-process and consensus-building skills are used;
- effective communication skills are used;
- there is effective use of technology to manage school operations;
- fiscal resources of the school are managed responsibly, efficiently, and effectively;
- a safe, clean, and aesthetically pleasing school environment is created and maintained;
- human resource functions support the attainment of school goals;
- confidentiality and privacy of school records are maintained.

Standard 4

A school administrator is an educational leader who promotes the success for all students by collaborating with families and community members, responding to diverse community interests, and needs, and mobilizing community resources.

The administrator has knowledge and understanding of

- emerging issues and trends that potentially impact the school community;
- the conditions and dynamics of the diverse school community;
- community resources;
- community relations and marketing strategies and processes;
- successful models of school, family, business, community, government and higher education partnerships.

The administrator believes in, values, and is committed to

- schools operating as an integral part of the larger community;
- collaboration and communication with families;
- involvement of families and other stakeholders in school decision-making processes;
- the proposition that diversity enriches the school;
- families as partners in the education of their children;
- the proposition that families have the best interests of their children in mind;
- resources of the family and community needing to be brought to bear on the education of students;
- an informed public.

The administrator facilitates processes and engages in activities ensuring that

- high visibility, active involvement, and communications with the larger community is a priority;
- relationships with community leaders are identified and nurtured;
- information about family and community concerns, expectations, and needs is used regularly;
- there is outreach to different business, religious, political, and service agencies and organizations;
- credence is given to individuals and groups whose values and opinions may conflict;
- the school and community serve one another as resources;
- available community resources are secured to help the school solve problems and achieve goals;
- partnerships are established with area businesses, institutions of higher education, and community groups to strengthen programs and support school goals;
- community youth family services are integrated with school programs;

- community stakeholders are treated equitably;
- diversity is recognized and valued;
- effective media relations are developed and maintained;
- a comprehensive program of community relations is established;
- public resources and funds are used appropriately and wisely;
- community collaboration is modeled for staff;
- opportunities for staff to develop collaborative skills are provided.

Standard 5

A school administrator is an educational leader who promotes the success of all students by acting with integrity, fairness, and in an ethical manner.

The administrator has knowledge and understanding of

- the purpose of education and the role of leadership in modern society;
- various ethical frameworks and perspectives on ethics;
- the values of the diverse school community;
- professional codes of ethics;
- the philosophy and history of education.

The administrator believes in, values, and is committed to

- the ideal of the common good;
- the principles in the Bill of Rights;
- the right of every student to a free, quality education;
- bringing ethical principles to the decision-making process;
- subordinating one's own interest to the good of the school community;
- accepting the consequences for upholding one's principles and actions;
- using the influence of one's office constructively and productively in the service of all students and their families;
- development of a caring school community.

The administrator

- examines personal and professional values;
- demonstrates a personal and professional code of ethics;
- demonstrates values, beliefs, and attitudes that inspire others to higher levels of performance;
- serves as a role model;
- accepts responsibility for school operations;
- considers the impact of one's administrative practices on others;
- uses the influence of the office to enhance the educational program rather than for personal gain;
- treats people fairly, equitable, and with dignity and respect;
- protects the rights and confidentiality of students and staff;
- demonstrates appreciation for and sensitivity to the diversity in the school community;

- recognizes and respects the legitimate authority of others;
- examines and considers the prevailing values of the diverse school community;
- expects that others in the school community will demonstrate integrity and exercise ethical behavior;
- opens the school to public scrutiny;
- fulfills legal and contractual obligations;
- applies laws and procedures fairly, wisely, and considerately.

Standard 6

A school administrator is an educational leader who promotes the success for all students by understanding, responding to, and influencing the larger political, social, economic, legal, and cultural context.

The administrator has knowledge and understanding of

- principles of representative governance that undergird the system of American schools;
- the role of public education in developing and renewing a democratic society and an economically productive nation;
- the law as related to education and schooling;
- the political, social, cultural and economic systems and processes that impact schools;
- models and strategies of change and conflict resolution as applied to the larger political, social, cultural and economic contexts of schooling;
- global issues and forces affecting teaching and learning;
- the dynamics of policy development and advocacy under our democratic political system;
- the importance of diversity and equity in a democratic society.

The administrator believes in, values, and is committed to

- education as a key to opportunity and social mobility;
- recognizing a variety of ideas, values, and cultures;
- importance of a continuing dialogue with other decision makers affecting education;
- actively participating in the political and policy-making context in the service of education;
- using legal systems to protect student rights and improve student opportunities.

The administrator facilitates processes and engages in activities ensuring that

- the environment in which schools operate is influenced on behalf of students and their families;
- communication occurs among the school community concerning trends, issues, and potential changes in the environment in which schools operate;

- there is ongoing dialogue with representatives of diverse community groups;
- the school community works within the framework of policies, laws, and regulations enacted by local, state, and federal authorities;
- public policy is shaped to provide quality education for students;
- lines of communication are developed with decision makers outside the school community.

References

Archer, J. (2007). The theory of action. *Education Week, 25,* 3, 53.

Bernhardt, V. L. (1994). *The school portfolio: A comprehensive framework for school improvement.* Princeton, NJ: Eye on Education.

Block, P. (1993). *Stewardship: Choosing service over self-interest.* San Francisco: Berrett-Koehler.

Collins, J. (2001). *Good to great.* New York: Harper Collins.

Chavez, C. (1992, April). Assessment in the learning organization: Shifting the paradigm. In A. Costa & B. Kallick (Eds.), *Address at the Annual Assessment Conference.* Alexandria, VA: Association for Supervision and Curriculum Development.

Darling-Hammond, L., & Sykes, G. (1999). *Teaching as the learning profession: Handbook of policy and practice.* San Francisco: Jossey-Bass.

Dietz, M. E. (1995). Using portfolios as a framework for professional development. *Journal of Staff Development, 16*(2), 40–43.

Dietz, M. E. (1999). Portfolios. *Journal of Staff Development, 20*(3), 45–46.

Dietz, M. E. (2007). *Journals as frameworks for professional learning communities.* Thousand Oaks, CA: Corwin Press.

Dietz, M. E., Barker, S., & Giberson, N. (2005). Solving a wicked problem. *Leadership, 34*(3), 20–23.

Dolan, W. P. (1994). *Restructuring our schools: A primer on systemic change.* Kansas City, MO: Systems and Organization.

DuFour, R., & Eaker, R. (1998). *Professional learning communities at work.* Alexandria, VA: Association for Supervision and Curriculum Development.

Fullan, M. (1991). *The new meaning of educational change.* New York: Teachers College Press.

Fullan, M. (2001). *Leading in a culture of change.* San Fransicso: Jossey-Bass.

Gardner, H. (1995, September 13). A cognitive view of leadership. *Education Week,* 34.

Glatthorn, A. A., Bragaw, D., Dawkins, K., & Parker, J. (1998). *Performance assessment and standards-based curricula: The achievement cycle.* Princeton, NJ: Eye on Education.

Glickman, C. D. (1993). *Renewing America's schools.* San Francisco: Jossey-Bass.

Graves, S. S. (1996). *An examination of the value of the professional development portfolio: A conceptual framework for professional growth.* Unpublished doctoral dissertation, College of Education, Ohio University.

Griffin, D., & Christensen, R. (1999). *Concerns-based adoption model (CBAM) levels of use of an innovation.* Denton, TX: Institute for the Integration of Technology into Teaching and Learning.

Horsley, D. L., & Loucks-Horsley, S. (1998). CBAM brings order to the tornado of change. *Journal of Staff Development, 19,* 4.

Interstate School Leaders Licensure Consortium. (1996). *Standards for school leaders* [Electronic version]. Washington, DC: Council of Chief State School Officers.

Jacobs, H. H. (1997). *Mapping the big picture: Integrating curriculum and assessment K–12.* Alexandria, VA: Association for Supervision and Curriculum Development.

Joyce, B., & Showers, B. (2002). *Student achievement through staff development.* Alexandria, VA: Association for Supervision and Curriculum Development.

Joyce, B., Wolf, J., & Calhoun, E. (1993). *The self-renewing school.* Alexandria, VA: Association for Supervision and Curriculum Development.

Lambert, L. (1998). *Building leadership capacity in schools.* Alexandria, VA: Association for Supervision and Curriculum Development.

Lambert, L., Collay, M., & Dietz, M. E. (1995). *The constructivist leader.* New York: Teachers College Press.

McCarthy, K. W. (1992). *The on-purpose person.* Colorado Springs, CO: Pinon.

Ouchi, S. (2003). *Making schools work.* New York: Simon and Schuster.

Owen, J., Cox, P., & Watkins, J. (1994). *Genuine reward: Community inquiry into connecting learning, teaching, and assessing.* Andover, MA: The Regional Laboratory.

Packer, A. (1992). Learning living: A blueprint for high performance. In *A SCANS Report for America 2000: The Secretary's Commission on Achieving Necessary Skills.* Washington, DC: U.S. Department of Labor.

Pearson, P. D. (1993). Standards and English language arts: A policy perspective. *Journal of Reading Behavior, 25*(4), 457–475.

Poplin, M. (1994). *Voices from the inside: A report on schooling from inside the classroom.* Claremont, CA: Institute for Education in Transformation at the Claremont Graduate School.

Senge, P. (1990). *The fifth discipline: The art and practice of learning organizations.* New York: Doubleday.

Sergiovanni, T. J. (1993). *Building community in schools.* San Francisco: Jossey-Bass.

Wagner, T. (2003, November 12). Beyond testing: The 7 disciplines for strengthening instruction. *Education Week.*

Wagner, T. (2006). Rigor on trial. *Education Week, 25,* 18, 28–29.

Wagner, T., Kegan, R., Laskow, L. L., Lemons, R. W., Garnier, J., Helsing, D., et al. (2006). Change leadership—A practical guide to transforming our schools. San Francisco: Jossey-Bass.

Wheatley, M. (1992). *Leadership and the new science.* San Francisco: Berrett-Koehler.

Wiggins, G., & McTighe, J. (1998). *Understanding by design.* Alexandria, VA: Association for Supervision and Curriculum Development.

Wolf, K., & Dietz, M. E. (1998). Teaching portfolios: Purposes and possibilities. *Teacher Education Quarterly, 25*(1), 9–22.

Index

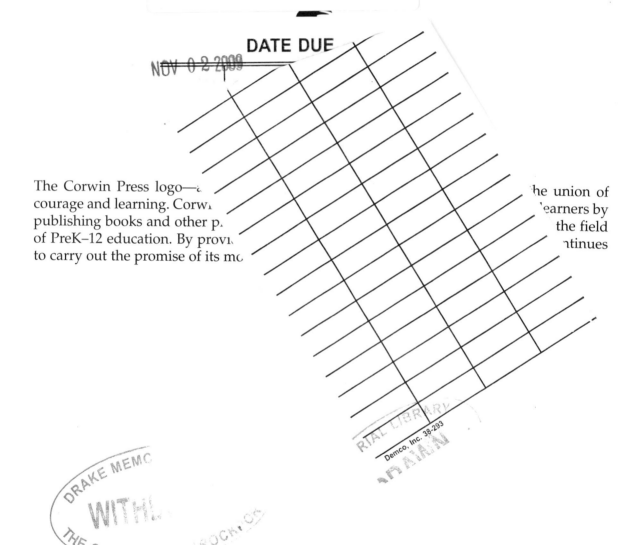

The Corwin Press logo—a ...   ...he union of
courage and learning. Corw...   ...earners by
publishing books and other p...   ...the field
of PreK–12 education. By provi...   ...ntinues
to carry out the promise of its mo...